How To Become A Consultant
In the Nonprofit & Charitable Sector

How To Become A Consultant
In the Nonprofit & Charitable Sector
By Carol Austin

Copyright © 2016 by Carol A. Austin

Published by Happy Press

Because of the dynamic nature of the Internet, any web addresses or links contained in this book may have changed since publication and may no longer be valid.

Cover Design by Jerry Dorris, Author Support

ISBN: 978-0-9958158-1-0

"Setting goals is the first step in turning the invisible into the visible."

– Anthony Robbins

Contents

INTRODUCTION

Imagine a career as a consultant where a typical day means you wake without an alarm clock, hit the yoga studio for a morning class, then work in your home office for about four hours (still in your comfy yoga clothes). Around four o'clock, you decant a bottle of Malbec and start prepping ingredients for a healthy, home-cooked meal.

When the snow flies in December, you take off for sunny Florida. You spend a couple of months as a snowbird and continue to "work from home." In July, you take a month off for vacation and travel to Europe or jump in the car for a road trip. Forget about those two or three short weeks your old employer gave you. Your time is flexible now. You are in complete control of when and for how long you can take a break.

At the end of the year, you earn anywhere from $50,000 to over $100,000—as well as benefit from home office tax deductions.

This is my life, and it can be yours too. Oh and I forgot to add—the work that you do is inspiring, fulfilling and creative. Things like...

...creating a new brand identity for an international

organization that helps children overcome the challenges of poverty

...revamping the content of a website and developing marketing materials for a local food bank

...organizing a fundraising event for a women's shelter.

Entrepreneurial self-employment is on the rise and thriving in the United States, Canada, and globally. At the same time, the voluntary sector—which comprises countless nonprofit and charitable organizations—is booming. Statistics on the size of this sector have been difficult to pin down, but thanks to efforts by The John Hopkins University, Center for Civil Society Studies, we have better information that can point us to countries where the most opportunities exist.

Voluntary sector organizations offer a wealth of rewarding work opportunities. And because of the way they are funded, they consistently contract outsourced services to freelance professionals. Consultants who are savvy enough to niche themselves and tap into this sector, have built fulfilling and lucrative careers with that dream combination of work-at-home and be-your-own-boss flexibility.

I am one of those consultants. I specialized my work in the nonprofit and charitable sector successfully for over 15 years. Over that time, many people have asked me how I did it. I've mentored a number of young and older entrepreneurs and helped them launch their own successful consulting practice in this rewarding sector. This book will explain the how-to— my experiences and insider strategies. I'll outline everything you need to consider—from whether this type of career is right for you, to specific resources and sage advice. More importantly, I'll give you some ideas on how you can make the transition from cubicle to consulting. Whether you are choosing your first career, transitioning to a new career, or considering an encore career later in life, you'll find helpful information on this wonderful niche sector.

Good luck in your new career!

Carol Austin

CHAPTER ONE
The Job Prospects

My average day goes like this: I wake around six or seven o'clock in the morning—no alarm clock needed. I start the day with morning tea on the couch and catch up on the overnight news on my iPad. I also use this time to check emails and address any quick issues from clients or other consultants I'm working with. After an hour of this leisurely start, I get dressed and head to the gym for a workout or yoga class. Or some days, I take a morning walk with my dog to get myself energized. By 9 or 10 am, I sit down at my computer and work for 4 hours or so until around 2 pm—depending on my current workload. At this point, I may relax by the pool or do some afternoon errands or grocery shopping. Sometimes in the evening after dinner, I'll answer a few more emails or do a little more work depending on deadlines. If I'm out of town and have any client meetings, I communicate by phone or by Skype. Some of my clients know that I escape to the South in the winter and they have no problem with that. Others are not aware of my location. I use an IP (Internet Protocol) phone line that uses my Toronto local number even while in the US.

Over the last decade, people have been embracing

entrepreneurship in record numbers. The role of technology has been the primary driving force along with the globalization of many business sectors. Large and small businesses have embraced a virtual environment where technology connects them easily to self-employed consultants. Other factors have played a significant role such as shifting attitudes about work-life balance, the affordability of home-based technologies, and an increasing awareness and interest in entrepreneurship. The baby boomer segment in particular has been one of the largest growing segments of the start-up market. Those 50 and over folks are highly educated, skilled, and have well-developed business networks.

As governments downsize their operations and large corporations look for cost-saving measures, outsourcing has become a normal practice. Strategic alliances are quickly and flexibly built between a company, small specialized businesses, and freelancers who take on a time-limited project. The group is dissolved once the work is done.

One of the most interesting niche markets for consultants is working for nonprofits and charities. Whether you are young and choosing your first career, or senior and exploring an encore career, this sector offers a wealth of rewarding work opportunities. It's ideal if you are the kind of person who longs for a job with meaning and purpose.

The nonprofit and charitable sector (also referred to as "the voluntary sector") is an economic force in a number of countries: the United States, Canada, Belgium, France, Japan, are a few examples. Contribution to GDP varies widely, but accounts for more than 5 percent of GDP in 6 of the 16 countries on which data are available (Canada, Israel, Mozambique, the United States, Belgium, New Zealand, and Japan). This makes the voluntary sector a sizeable part of the economy in these countries, similar in scope to industries like transportation, agriculture, utilities and construction. *(Lester M. Salamon, et al, The State of Global Civil Society and Volunteering: Latest findings from the implementation of the UN Nonprofit Handbook. Working Paper No. 49. Johns Hopkins Center for Civil Society Studies, 2013.)*

These organizations are everywhere. We all engage with them on a regular basis, from small community service organizations to large hospitals and universities. The sector also includes services in arts and culture, religion, sports, recreation, civic advocacy, environmental protection, and a variety of business, labour, and professional associations.

Charities and nonprofits are funded by a variety of sources including income from the sale of products and services, individual or corporate donations, and government funding and foundation grants. As a result, many of these organizations never know from one year to the next, what funding dollars they will have to run their operations. Dollars earmarked as *core funding* are used to maintain core full-time staff, while *project funding* is applied to one-time projects or development work. Some organizations are largely volunteer-driven.

Because of this tenuous funding model, many organizations rely on time-limited contracts or a project approach to getting the work done. Outsourcing to freelance consultants is an effective way for these organizations to avoid committing to full-time staff that they may not be able to sustain over the long term. For example, consultants are ideally suited to special-event coordination and targeted fundraising campaigns. High quality consulting strengthens an organization over the long term in a multitude of ways.

In addition, a good consultant brings great value to nonprofit and charitable organizations. The result of a successful consulting engagement usually means a long-overdue project gets completed on schedule. Consultants bring diverse skills, best practices, and an outside perspective. They encourage team approaches to getting the work done. A good consultant helps an organization develop the internal skills to eventually carry out a new development area themselves. The very best consultants strengthen an organization over the long term.

Nonprofits Versus Charities

If the voluntary sector is new to you, it's important that you understand the difference between a nonprofit and a charity. All charities are nonprofits, but not all nonprofits are charities.

A nonprofit is based on the simple premise that none of the organization's net profit from donations, membership fees, or any kind of business activities will benefit the organization or any individual. Nonprofits do not need to operate exclusively for charitable purposes—they can operate for social welfare, civic improvement, pleasure, sport, recreation or any other purpose except for profit.

Charities, on the other hand, must be registered and approved by governing taxation agencies in their home country. Generally, they must be established and operate exclusively for charitable purposes that benefit the general public. Examples are churches, educational organizations, hospitals, and some government units.

Technical characteristics that also separate charities from other nonprofits are the kinds of tax returns a charity is required to file. Charities can also issue official donation receipts while nonprofits cannot.

Depending on the country you plan to work for, it's important to research and understand the difference between nonprofits, charities, foundations, and other governmental or quasi-governmental agencies. This is especially relevant if you consult in areas such as grant writing or fundraising where you will need to know the rules around official donation receipts. Also in the area of grant writing, you'll quickly discover that many funding sources have a strict eligibility requirement that applicant organizations be registered charities. Some nonprofit organizations get around this by working under the umbrella of a registered charity.

CHAPTER TWO
Consulting in the Voluntary Sector

The term "consulting" is not really the best word to describe this line of work because it may imply a person who merely offers business advice. This can be true in the case of high-end management consultants from organizations like Deloitte Touche or Ernst and Young. That category of consultants are generally savvy MBA's who apply complex business solutions to large corporations. This book focuses on the type of consultants who are small business freelancers —and the work involves *both* advising and executing the work.

The focus of this book as a niche consultant is not only important for people seeking meaningful and purposeful careers, but it's an important selling tool for building a business. The concept is known as niche marketing and the logic behind it seems to go against what you normally might think makes sense when building a business. When considering a consulting practice, you might think it's best to hang a shingle as a consultant and target every possible organization whether for-profit or nonprofit. But there are problems with this and here's a few reasons why niche marketing and developing a specialized service can generate more business for you:

1. There's less competition and you'll stand out from the crowd.

2. It's easier to tailor your message and services in your marketing.

3. Clients are highly attracted to someone with a deep understanding of their needs.

4. You'll get referred more often when people know what you do.

If you're still not convinced, you can research the concept of niche marketing to learn more. If you are convinced and ready to dive in, then let's talk more specifically about consulting for nonprofits and charities and what that means. If you already work for a voluntary sector organization, you can likely skip this chapter. If you're new to the sector, you need to start understanding the unique needs of these organizations and what will eventually set you apart as a niche consultant.

So What's Unique About The Sector?

Like all corporations, nonprofits and charities are entrepreneurial in nature. The key difference is in their bottom line—which is NOT making money for profit or shareholder gain. Nonprofits and charities are on a constant quest to advance their cause, increase donations, make change, and ultimately, to help people and communities in some way. To that end, they are also driven to function more professionally. In fact, over the past few years, there's been a major shift in the voluntary sector largely driven by the expectations of funding bodies. As the demand for funding dollars gets more and more competitive, funders insist that organizations follow corporate-style best practices in how they operate. Increasingly greater attention is given to areas such as board governance, performance measures, and effective workflow processes. For-profit corporations have also influenced the sector in the recent past as companies jump on the trend toward increased corporate social responsibility. As a result, these for-profit sponsors hold high standards for the charities they choose to support.

Generally speaking, many nonprofits and charities are staffed by people passionate about the cause they serve which may include original founders and long-time volunteers turned employees. Consultants enter the picture with a broad range of experience from multiple sectors. They are able to bring an innovative, professional, and best practices approach to the work.

All nonprofits and charities are managed at the top by a Board of Directors. Boards can include anywhere from 3 to 20 people all of whom come from a diverse background and provide a variety of perspectives. Their influence may also drive the hiring of consultants since many board members are professionals, executives, or academics who understand the importance of hiring skilled external expertise.

The bottom line for a charity or nonprofit is the realization of a social mission—not dollars and cents. This is often the biggest challenge for leadership and management to wrap their heads around. Establishing the right programs, measuring progress, and setting priorities is not as straightforward as it is for profit-driven organizations.

Consultants in this sector must recognize how this kind of value-driven model impacts the deliverables they craft for an organization.

The unique dynamic of nonprofits and charities—from their funding model to their planning needs—provides endless opportunities for consulting work, but it's also important to understand that it shapes the work you'll do and how you should approach it. These organizations will look to you to bring a high level of knowledge of the sector, new ideas, best practices, and current trends. As a consultant, you are selling yourself, and the more experience you bring to the table, the more marketable you'll be.

In most cases, working as a consultant means responding to a "Request For Proposal" or "RFP" for short, from a nonprofit or charity. It might also mean working alongside another consultant who has been awarded a contract through an RFP process. The organization will have some kind of strategic issue they are grappling with or a project to be carried out. As a consultant, you will be required to help the client clearly flesh out what is needed for the task at hand and then propose solutions that will meet that need. You will likely then participate in the actual carrying out of that task.

The following is just a partial list of some of the areas where consultants are frequently hired by nonprofit and charitable organizations. These areas will be described in more detail in the chapter on specialization, which will give you a better idea of the specific kinds of things you might do as a consultant. Some of these functional areas are unique to nonprofits and charities, but others are similar or cross-functional to for-profit organizations. Having or developing an understanding of how these areas differ in the voluntary sector is what will ultimate set you apart as a niche consultant.

- Fundraising

- Grant writing

- Strategic Planning

- Board Governance Training

- Facilitation

- Technology

- Marketing & Communications

- Web and Social Media

- Volunteer Coordination

- Project Management

Once you have completed the project you've been hired to do, there is usually some type of reporting component—usually in the form of a written report, but sometimes as both a written report and a verbal presentation. Working for a new client usually means that you will have additional work in the future from this same client—especially if you've done a good job. Acquiring a new client can take a considerable amount of effort at the outset, but it usually means you'll have a client for the life of your career.

Depending on the area you plan to specialize in, you'll find other unique ways in which nonprofits and charities function (and struggle)—all impacting upon what you do:

- Staffing is often highly diverse.

- Small nonprofits never have enough time, staffing or funds to do what is needed.

- Attracting and retaining good managers and executives may be hard due to insufficient funds.

- Executive leadership wear too many hats.

- Technology may be poor due to a lack of proper funding or dedicated staff in this area.

- Strategic planning may be non-existent or lack a structured process.

- Boards of Directors are often dysfunctional and lacking in proper governance training.

- Organizations often fail to understand or implement proper measurement and performance indicators.

The good thing for consultants, is that the vast majority of nonprofits and charities need so much help There's a ton of rewarding work to sink your teeth into. Hiring a consultant is a cost-effective and efficient way for these organizations to advance their work. The opportunities are there for you.

CHAPTER THREE
The Pros and Cons of Consulting

Sometimes the grass is greener on the other side, so before you go quitting your full-time job, you should seriously think about the downsides of consulting and make sure the benefits outweigh any risks for you. We'll explore the pros and cons first, and then we'll consider whether you personally have what it takes to be a consultant. Being a consultant means being an entrepreneur, which can be exciting and appealing. Entrepreneurs have the power to create their own opportunities, and the possibilities can be endless. You can work where you like and work with people you like. You can choose the kind of work you enjoy doing, and you can really feel like you are making a difference. This is especially true in the nonprofit and charitable sector where the work is fulfilling and either community-based or globally-based. However, not everyone is suited to self-employment so be careful to weigh the pros and cons before diving in.

The Negatives

First off, say goodbye to that regular paycheque. Being self-employed means sometimes going for a long period of time without any income while other times having more money than you know what to do with. There is a feeling of insecurity with that kind of instability. For some people, this can be quite stressful and just doesn't work for their personality or financial and personal situation.

Working as a consultant means always having to hustle and create new sales opportunities—especially in the early stages of building up a consulting practice. A portion of your time will go towards marketing your business, answering RFPs, and networking and training—all time that is unpaid. It can be difficult spending 20 hours developing a proposal, getting shortlisted and giving a killer proposal presentation, only to be rejected in the end. You have to be thick-skinned and move on to the next opportunity, knowing you have what it takes to land enough work each year.

Depending on the type of work you will do, consulting can be somewhat isolating. Most consultants work from home where the only work colleague is the family dog. There are ways to balance this like working one or two days a week at a client site, maintaining regular networking lunches with friends, clients or colleagues, or participating in online discussion groups on various topics of professional interest. No matter what, being self-employed will never be the same as a regular five-day-a-week office job where you develop long-term working relationships with a consistent group of people.

The Positives

The flip-side of not having a regular paycheque is that the earning potential for a consultant is both unlimited and potentially lucrative. Depending on your skills and experience, how hard you want to work, and how much work you can juggle at once, you can pretty much count on a comfortable yearly income. The range for most consultants specializing in the voluntary sector is a gross income of $50,000 to $100,000 a year. Consultants who network with other contractors to build a team or small agency can garner higher profits.

Being self-employed also means you can benefit from home office tax deductions which include your equipment and supplies, transportation costs, and a portion of your total housing costs. There's other small savings too that can add up. Things like reduced commuting costs, less money spent on a business wardrobe, and less money spent on work-day lunches eating in restaurants.

The best thing about consulting work is the flexibility in work hours and the control over your work effort. If you'd like to take a morning fitness class, help out on your child's next school trip, or take a day off for a hike with nature, go right ahead. You have no one to answer to but yourself. If you like working in the evenings and sleeping in late, that works just fine too. Consulting is also a fantastic encore career for older workers who are leaving the traditional workforce, but not quite ready to retire.

The most important benefit in self-employment is the potential positive effect on health and family life. For today's typical busy household of two-income earners, it's a tremendous bonus for a family if one person can work from home. Quite often, you can work less hours and still make the same amount of money as a salaried job—yet have time to cook healthy family meals and raise young children or help with grandchildren. In addition to savings in commuting costs, clothing costs, and tax benefits, being home in the afternoon might mean no daycare costs. When you sit down to analyze the financial case for becoming a consultant, remember to include these potential savings in the equation. The increase in quality of life for you, your children, and your partner is a persuasive argument for launching a career as a consultant.

CHAPTER FOUR
Do You Have What It Takes?

Not everyone is cut out for consulting work. The appeal of being self-employed may be your primary motivating factor, but you need to take a hard look at whether you have what it takes right now, or can work toward self-improvement in these areas. You can certainly learn as you go along, but having a good portion of these abilities from the start makes sense.

If you are young and only just starting your career with the hope of someday being a consultant, there are things you can begin to do now to help build well-rounded skills. Sign up for evening courses in continuing education on some of the topics outlined in this chapter. If you work for a fairly large employer, make sure you don't stagnate in your job. If you feel bored or unchallenged, seek out new opportunities within the organization. A new role will expose you to new skill areas and constantly push you to learn. If you've exhausted opportunities at your current job, consider moving to another organization. If your employer offers extracurricular activities or team working groups, raise your hand whenever they are offered. If your place of employment is simply not challenging, get involved in the community and volunteer with an organization that needs help. Volunteer roles provide great opportunities for taking on a level of responsibility you might not get with your employer. Just remember, if you're not feeling challenged, you're probably not learning.

In the early years of my career-building, I always stayed active at the community level. In my twenties, I founded a community food cooperative that grew to include over 50 families in my New York City neighbourhood where I was living at the time. The skills I developed doing this were invaluable. Things like project management, financial record keeping, and volunteer management—areas that at the time I was not doing in my day job. Another community role during this period was working in partnership with a small group of parents to develop a community daycare. Later on in my thirties when I had moved back to Toronto, I was active in my local church as a member of the church's Board of Directors. I managed areas such as facilities, human resources, and programming. I've been a condominium board member on two separate occasions, volunteered at the Royal Ontario Museum working with children, and have built websites for local choirs and other arts groups. All of my volunteer work over the years exposed me to skill building that was 100% free, on-the-job training that is now highly marketable and relevant in the work I do as a consultant.

If you are older, nearing retirement and now looking for an encore career, you likely have extensive skills not only from your working life, but your personal life. The nice thing about consulting is that you are not confined by the limits of your resume. Experiences in your personal life such as raising children and dealing with the education system, owning real estate and renovating properties, travel, financial and estate planning, and so many other aspects of everyday life, can influence marketable skill areas you never knew you had.

Let's take a look at some of the key personal and skill areas that are important in assessing your potential as a consultant.

Personal Financial Management

As I mentioned in the previous chapter, there are some important considerations in the area of finances—specifically, how well you manage your money and your tolerance for high and low periods of income generation.

Working as a consultant means you can't always count on a regular paycheque unless you have some kind of long-term assignment with a steady client. Especially in the start-up phase, you may go for an extended period of time without any income. The way I handle these dry periods is to have a line of credit tied to my bank account. When work is lean or clients haven't paid me on time, I use my credit line for regular bills. When income comes in, I pay off the credit line in full.

You'll also need to avoid the temptation to go on a spending spree when you suddenly get a large client payment. Being a good money manager means living within your means and budgeting wisely—important habits no matter what your career choice is. This kind of planning is even more important when you are self-employed. A good approach is to create a simple annual business plan for yourself.   Determine the net annual income you need to support your lifestyle. Use a monthly budget spreadsheet to come up with the annual amount. Then work backward and consider the number of contracts you need to secure for the year to meet your income goals. You can include other goals in your business plan such as monthly targets for proposals, client meetings, or networking opportunities—goals that will keep you active and on track each month.

Self-Direction and Discipline

Your level of personal discipline is an important attribute because you most definitely need to be self-directed and disciplined with your time in any self-employed business. Working at home can mean lots of distractions. The good thing is that there are usually plenty of client deadlines to keep you on track. However, you still need to map out each week and think about the work you need to get done, breaking things down into daily tasks. If you are the type of person who has trouble staying focused or motivated, you might not be a good candidate for self-employment.

On the flip side, you also don't want to fall into the trap of being a workaholic. The best approach is to have a business plan up-front and know what your earning requirements are each year. Then you can break this down into monthly, weekly, then daily work requirements. The whole point of being self-employed is to have work-life balance, so if you have a ton of work coming your way, be careful to manage it sensibly.

If your consulting practice ends up growing by leaps and bounds, another option is to subcontract some of the work to other consultants or juniors. You can also employ family members. Just be sure to have them give you an invoice because you can deduct those costs as legitimate business expenses.

Organizational Skills

Discipline and organization go hand-in-hand. It's almost impossible to have good discipline without being organized. That means knowing how to prioritize work properly, and working quickly and efficiently. As a consultant, you want to find the right balance between delivering high quality work in the least amount of time. Time is money and you need to get faster and better at what you do as time goes on. Make use of either paper or technology tools like online calendars and reminder systems. If you prefer paper-based tools, buy yourself a good agenda book to keep track of appointments, notes, and to-do lists. Use file folders to mark client files and keep paper-based resources at hand. Set up electronic file folders on your computer in an organized fashion—one named for each client, with sub-folders for client projects. Also organize your own business files in folders and keep track of work samples, proposal templates, and signed contracts. This will make it easier to quickly respond to RFP's.

Good organizational skills also means a strong attention to detail. If you want to please your clients and continually attract new work by building a good reputation as a consultant, you need to produce high quality work that is well organized and thorough.

Here's my simple method for staying organized. I've worked this way for years now. It's a great way to juggle multiple clients and demands, as well as the many details of my personal life. Are you ready because it's very simple and low-tech. I use a single notebook—about 8" x 6" in size with a spiral binding so it lies flat when open (this is important— avoid the hardbound notebooks that look nice, but don't lay flat). I don't like smaller notebooks and I don't like the large 8-1/2" x 11" size because those are too big on my desk. My notebook sits open in front of me at all times when I'm working. I rarely use other notepads or sticky notes unless I have some critical reminder that I need to stick up on my computer.

Now here's the important steps: Into this notepad goes everything going on in my life—notes scribbled while on a call with a client, research notes, personal to-do lists, work to-do lists, phone numbers, and meeting notes. The most critical next step is the simple to-do list. Every evening, morning or every couple of days (whatever feels right to you)—open to a clean page in your notebook and make a to- do list of the things you need to address.

My personal work ethic includes listening very carefully to what a client needs from me and always following through on what I said I would do. Add those details to my busy family life and I can always chime off a to-do list. Sometimes my lists are a mixture of client and personal work, but often I'll separate items into different categories. I also put some to-do items into online reminder apps, but I find that things move so quickly in my life that paper works better for me. (For a great online list-making system, check out Wunderlist.)

The notebook method works really well because I simply flip back through my scribbled pages and find items that I need to do. When I no longer need the information on one of the pages, I put a diagonal cross through the page to mark that I'm done with everything on that page. If there is something critical on that page that I still need to reference, I'll leave it uncrossed and put a box around the information. Sometimes I'll dog-ear that page as well.

Once I go through past pages and create my to-do list, I feel confident that I haven't missed some important detail— especially a client-related item. When I attend client meetings, I take my notebook with me (unless I'm using my laptop for more detailed notes), open to a clean page, and write the client name and date at the top before jotting my meeting notes. I fill up these notebooks usually within about 2 to 3 months. I then keep the old books on a shelf usually for a year before discarding them. Sometimes there is something I need to reference and I know I'll find it in one of my trusty notebooks.

Writing Skills

As a consultant, good business writing skills are a must-have. If you are not a good writer, yet committed to starting a consulting practice, this is one area you will need to develop. Most consultants are writing all the time and drafting a wide variety of document types including proposals, statements of work (SOWs), research papers, strategy reports, planning briefs, slide presentations, grants, and so many other documents.

Emails or any other general communications to your clients also need to be well written and professional. These types of messages should be clear, concise, and intelligent. Your writing voice in emails should always be business-like.

Avoid casual colloquialisms, emoticons, or elaborate email stationery. Always proofread your emails and other writing. As a strong writer, you also need to produce work quickly to maximize productivity. Being a confident writer is critical.

There could be some consulting areas where you may not do as much writing—for example, if you specialize in organizing fundraising events or doing primarily technical work such as websites. However, in most cases, writing will be a big part of your job. If you specialize in any area relating to marketing, communications and public relations, your writing skills will need to be at an advanced level. If you need to brush up your writing skills, find a local course on business-writing skills. Invest in some good writing reference books and teach yourself good proofreading habits.

A Learning Personality

If you have a learning personality, you will be well suited to consulting work. A learning personality is someone who has a natural passion for learning. Think of consulting as getting a new job every few months. In any new job, there is always an initial period known as "the learning curve".   Most employers are fairly forgiving during this period as a new employee ramps up to acquire the necessary institutional and job knowledge. For a skilled consultant though, this learning curve should be minimal to none. The quicker you can step into a client environment and grasp what is needed, the more desirable your services will be.

If you possess a natural learning personality to begin with, there are some tricks to getting through this learning curve quite easily. First of all, you'll have the Internet at your fingertips. Being a consultant in the age of the Internet is much easier than it was 40 years ago. If you are not already an expert in the topic area or sector where you're about to do some work, then you need to get on the Internet and research it until you get there. You can also make use of your local library and stock up on relevant books on the topic area. These research and learning skills also come into play once you start the actual work for your client. You'll usually be handed a tall stack of background documents on the organization or on the issue they are dealing with. You'll need to quickly get through this information and distill the most relevant content for the work you are doing. You'll be highlighting and taking notes, so your academic note-taking skills will be important here. Depending on the work you are doing, you might produce research data or other information in the course of the work, which you'll again need to distill for the client into recommendations and reports.

A learning personality also includes strong analytical skills. You need to grasp the client's "pain points" and use your experience and knowledge within the sector to develop appropriate strategies to address those issues. Over time you will become an expert at this both from a business sense and within the voluntary sector itself. This will become an important marketing attribute as you hold yourself out as an expert in the sector.

Communication Skills

Communication skills are an obvious trait to mention here, but it's an important area to emphasize. As a consultant you need to be articulate and to communicate well. You'll be called upon to sell yourself as well as your knowledge and experience—especially in the early stages of working with a client. Later, you'll need to provide your opinion and advice in a credible and confident manner. You may have to give a verbal report or chair a team meeting so public speaking skills and a strong vocabulary are important skills to develop.

Included in the category of communication skills are strong active listening skills. It's critically important to always listen carefully to what your client, other staff, and other stakeholders are telling you. This verbal information will inform everything you do. Good communications are critical as you address issues, educate, guide, and innovate throughout the process. As a consultant you want to avoid making any errors in your work or to find yourself in a position where you are not doing what you should be doing because you didn't listen carefully enough. Throughout your client engagements, you will also be dealing with a wide variety of people at all levels of an organization including administrative staff, middle managers, senior managers, and board members. An ability to communicate with confidence and authority at all levels will allow you to gain trust and credibility with these stakeholders.

If you plan to specialize in areas such as training or facilitation, your communication skills will need to be at an advanced level. If you don't already have these skills, you should seek out further professional development through local training courses. A wonderful resource to tap into is Toastmasters which offers an inexpensive and fun way to develop communication and leadership skills.

Technical Skills

Being a consultant means being somewhat of a Jack or Jill of all trades. You might be a good writer or a good communicator, but how good are your word processing skills? Do you know how to use PowerPoint and Excel? Especially today in our highly technological world, the more you know or can learn, the easier your job will be and the greater value you'll bring to client work. The other option is to pay someone else to handle these administrative tasks for you. However, if you are just starting out, this is likely not an option. You will also find that some organizations you work for will be extremely advanced in their use of technology while others will be dragging behind the times. This is not unusual for smaller cash-strapped nonprofits and charities.

If you are not already skilled using today's most common software packages such as Microsoft Office, consider finding some local courses to help you cover at least the basics. Internet research skills are also critically important. If you don't already use the Internet all the time (which many of us do), you should practice and get good at conducting Internet research. Things like: choosing the right keywords, narrowing topics, finding authoritative sources, and using multiple search engines are some steps for good research. Wiki How has a great page on conducting Internet research here: http://www.wikihow.com/Do-Internet-Research

Be aware also that some clients might have internal software systems that you will be required to use. Some examples are project management software, document collaboration tools, intranets, calendar and email software, or accounting systems. Many clients will provide training on these tools, but as much as possible, you need to embrace these technologies.

If you plan on specializing in technical areas such as

databases, web content management, social media marketing, or event coordination, your technical skills will need to be at an advanced level. If you don't already have these skills, you can seek out further professional development through local training courses.

An Entrepreneurial Attitude

Having an entrepreneurial attitude will impact two sides of your ability to be successful as a consultant—running and promoting your own business, and acting as a consultant for other organizations. Both areas will benefit if you have a natural entrepreneurial spirit. Reading this book is your first step down the path to becoming an entrepreneur. Once you delve into formulating your new career—which will include marketing yourself and attracting clients—you will tap into creative ideas and you will take risks. Working with clients, you will also need to be creative, a bit of a risk-taker, innovative, and tactical. These are all skills that are entrepreneurial in nature.

CHAPTER FIVE
Skill Development & Training

The ideal way to start a new career consulting in this sector, is to transition from a full-time job with a number of years of experience under your belt specifically in the voluntary sector. If you're not working in the sector already and you'd like to move into that area, it would make sense to work for at least six months to a year in a contract or permanent role with a nonprofit or charity, depending on how quickly you learn. On the job experience is the best way to acquire the necessary skills and to understand the functions, challenges, and workflows that are unique to nonprofits and charities. If you're a seasoned professional in the private sector, you will most definitely have many cross-functional skills. However, you will need to do some research or get some kind of exposure to the charity world in order to understand the subtle differences between these two environments.

If you are already working with a small or medium sized charity, you will likely have been exposed to a variety of skill areas. If you've changed jobs a couple of times within the sector, that's even better, since your experience will have more breadth. If you are now considering a career as a consultant, your first step is to sit down and do a thorough self-assessment of all of the different functional areas you have been exposed to over your career. Things like volunteer engagement or volunteer management, program management, marketing or public relations, grant or proposal writing, policy development, technology, working with boards or committees, event management or fundraising.

Next, continuing your self-assessment, list as many professional development and training opportunities you have had in your past jobs—no matter whether these were lengthy trainings or one-day trainings. What kind of technology tools have you used? When you consider all the things you've done, what are you best at and what gives you the most satisfaction and fulfillment in your work? All of this information and self-assessment work will be extremely helpful when you begin crafting your Curriculum Vitae (CV) and thinking about the areas you'd like to specialize in for your particular consulting practice.

After performing this self-assessment, consider any new training and development you might need by identifying the gaps in your knowledge and experience. Also consider the areas that interest you most. Perhaps you've done a bit of marketing and public relations here and there, and doing more of that really interests you. You can then check out some marketing and communications courses to bring your knowledge up to a professional level. Or maybe you'd like to get into web content management—you're a good writer and you like technology—but you know you need to learn HTML and CSS coding. If so, then you should seek out a training course on HTML/CSS or find online training to advance this skill.

If you have zero experience in the sector and you are early in your career and trying to break into this area—with the long-term goal of becoming a consultant—here's a few ideas to get you started.

Over the past few years, colleges have started offering certificate programs in nonprofit administration and management—recognizing the growing need within the sector and healthy job prospects. Consider one of these programs either full or part time depending on your schedule. Most of these programs include job placements and internships which gives you the extra benefit of on-the-job training and building networks.

Another thing to keep in mind is that entry-level jobs at nonprofits and charities are like any other job—you don't necessarily need any experience in the sector. So try to get your foot in the door by focusing your job search in the nonprofit sector only instead of the for-profit sector. If you work hard and prove your potential, it's often much easier to advance within these types of organizations versus corporate environments. For-profit organizations tend to draw a strict line between administrative staff and credentialed staff, whereas nonprofits and charities tend to be more open to growth from within.

Another great way to round out your experience in the voluntary sector, regardless of how much previous experience you have, is to volunteer with an organization that interests you. While of course there is no pay, you can instantly find yourself doing the actual work you would like to one day get paid for. Nonprofits and charities are always looking for volunteers, so this is a great way to get free training and acquire new skills. Years ago when I had only a little bit of grant writing work and wanted to do more, I volunteered one day a week for a Toronto-based arts foundation. They had me researching foundation and grant opportunities and writing up one-page summaries for their Board members to review. It was fantastic experience that served me well in later consulting work. These volunteer gigs also offer important networking opportunities. Some volunteer jobs can also lead to paid work. Once you solidify your career as a consultant, consider always having at least one client that you provide work to "pro bono". These opportunities will always provide value since you'll continue to hone new skills and add to your network of connections.

Professional Development
& Training Resources

Charity Village: www.charityvillage.com

Charity Village is the Canadian nonprofit sector's largest and most popular online resource for recruiting, sector news, and professional development information. I'll refer you to this site in a later chapter on finding work opportunities, but it is also a great site for training and development resources. Check out the eLearning tab for online courses, a directory of conferences and seminars, and a complete listing of post-secondary nonprofit programs in Canada.

Association of Fundraising Professionals: www.afpnet.org plus local chapters

The AFP is a global organization with about 30,000 members worldwide and local chapters that serve members directly. Canada has over 20 local chapters and the US has over 180 across the country. Check out the website for links to online chapter sites where you'll find training courses, conferences, and tons of great resources for professional development in the area of fundraising.

Volunteer Canada: www.volunteer.ca

Volunteer Canada provides a national voice for volunteerism and volunteer centres in Canada. It has provided leadership on issues and trends in the Canadian volunteer movement since 1977. Its website includes research, training and information on volunteer management, board volunteering, family volunteering, recognition, screening, youth volunteering, older adult volunteering and directors' and officers' insurance.

Ryerson University Centre for Voluntary Sector Studies: www.ryerson.ca/cvss/
This Centre aims to enhance understanding of the voluntary sector through research and education. There's a number of interesting resources here including the Nonprofit Job Market Study and links to symposiums and workshop events.

Nonprofit Technology Network (NTEN): www.nten.org
NTEN offers membership, networking, training, and a fantastic annual conference that you won't want to miss if the area of technology consulting interests you.

Idealist: www.idealist.org and idealistcareers.org
Idealist is a global nonprofit that helps purpose-driven professionals find, land, and love their social impact jobs. Visit both sites for information on Grad Fairs and nonprofit career resources and training.

US State Nonprofit Associations: www.councilofnonprofits.org/find-your-state-association
In the US, each state has a local Nonprofit Association and many provide things like peer networks, trainings for nonprofit leaders, and workshops on a variety of topics of interest for career-seekers. Visit the Council of Nonprofits for a link to a directory of all state associations.

CHAPTER SIX
Areas of Specialization

Now that you've completed a thorough self-assessment of your skills and interest, it is time to consider whether you plan to work as a *generalist* consultant or to specialize in a particular area. When you are first starting out as a consultant, out of necessity, you probably will need to go after as many different consulting opportunities as you can. Over time as you build up your client list, you'll be able to focus on the niche areas that interest you most. Niching your consultant area can be extremely beneficial when you are ready and able to do that. Essentially you'll be creating a niche within a niche – for example a facilitation expert in the nonprofit sector or a marketing specialist in the nonprofit sector. These are highly sought-after skills that will make you extremely marketable. This chapter outlines a few of the most common specialty areas in voluntary sector consulting so you can begin to think about where you'd like to specialize.

Fundraising Consultant

Fundraising consulting is one of the major areas of specialization for a consultant in the voluntary sector. Just about every organization within the sector has some element of fund development needs, except perhaps for organizations that are 100% volunteer run. There's a wide range of activities that fall under fundraising consulting including such areas as: recruiting and training volunteers, identifying new funding opportunities, developing new campaigns and managing existing campaigns, managing fundraising special events, or conducting direct major gift asks. Knowledge in the leading software called Raiser's Edge by Blackbaud is a good skill to learn for consultants interested in specializing as a fundraising consultant.

Note that fundraising consultancy ranges from high-level advice to hands-on technical management—and the fee range between those two categories varies widely. Providing high-level advice is only possible once you've acquired a few years of experience doing this kind of work—or have specialized training in this area. As a result, some top fundraising consultants can demand high fees. At this level, a consultant is usually brought in when an organization is struggling to increase its funding base and needs new ideas and strategies to help it move development goals toward a new direction. The consultant analyses the situation and comes up with a fundraising plan or strategy. This type of consulting is self-directed.

At the other end of the spectrum, consultants can be hired as freelance contractors to carry out very specific fundraising campaigns—for example, a special event like an annual gala or a run/walk campaign. This kind of work would be client-directed and you would be carrying out specific client plans and related tasks.

Event Management

Event management consulting may or may not be fundraising related. Some examples of non-fundraising events might be an educational conference or a volunteer recognition event. In either case, these events are usually large scale and involve detailed project management steps including: developing an event plan, hiring staff and volunteers, sourcing and contracting the appropriate venue along with audio-visual needs, arranging table rentals and catering, managing invitations and mailing lists, managing attendees and ticketing, and then managing the actual event. If the event is a conference, tasks would involve managing the program, speakers and agendas. Throughout these events, the consultant would be managing a financial budget, and at the end of the event, overseeing evaluation and measurement of results. This kind of work is perfect for someone who is detail oriented, high energy, and able to manage a high level of stress with ease.

Grant Writing

Grant writing could technically fall under the umbrella of fundraising, but it really is a separate skill area all its own. The process involved in a typical grant proposal is extensive and includes these activities:

- sourcing grant opportunities that properly match the needs of an organization and its projects;

- communicating with the granting or funding body to confirm the match and appropriateness of a grant proposal (this can greatly increase chances for success, although it's not always possible with all funding bodies, but is critical for those that allow it);

- advising the client on how best to shape the business strategy for the grant proposal and fleshing out the project;

- conducting any research required as input into the proposal;

- writing the grant;

- assisting with budget development for the project;

- finalizing the grant by assuring that all steps and fine details required by the granting body are followed to the letter;

- providing any supplementary information required by the granting body;

- managing an annual calendar of grant submissions; and

- managing the drafting and submission of reporting documents.

Depending on the size of the organization and the grant dollars sought, grant writing can be a complex and involved specialty area well suited to someone with these particular abilities: excellent writing skills, efficient research skills, strategy development skills, and attention to detail. A sub-area of grant writing is the drafting of proposal or funding letters to non-granting bodies such as corporate funders.

A word of advice when developing a consulting practice as a grant writer—be sure to focus on organizations that are well-established and have already had some success in acquiring grant or foundation dollars. Many people will approach a grant writer with A Great Idea to start a new charity assuming this automatically qualifies them for a grant. The problem is these people don't know the first thing about starting a nonprofit or charity venture and haven't done any research on what's involved in starting one. They also don't realize there are likely charities already doing the great idea. If you start down a path with them, you'll end up giving way too much of your valuable expertise and time helping them do business development and strategy work. They also most likely won't have any idea on what the grant opportunities are. If you get hired to do this type of research for someone, make sure you are getting paid by the hour, because the time spent on this can be enormous. This kind of work also falls into business development and strategic planning, and if that doesn't interest you, it's best to tell them to go off and do that work first before contacting you to write the actual grant.

Final words of advice for grant writers, never agree to be paid a commission based on whether or not a grant is successful in securing funds. For one thing, your time spent should always be compensated, and secondly, you do not have full control over whether someone has a bad idea and insists on pitching a grant proposal. What you can do is keep track of your grant outcomes—amounts you have helped secure for clients over the years. Use these outcomes to sell your worth to new clients.

Strategic Planning

Business development including the area of strategic planning can be interesting and rewarding work—especially if you are a big-picture thinker. To understand the potential consulting opportunities for supporting strategic planning activities, you need to understand how nonprofits and charities approach high level planning. Over the past 20 years or so, small to medium sized organizations have begun to use the same business best practices employed by larger organizations. This involves a process-driven approach and methodology. Key stakeholders of the organization (usually board members and senior staff) are brought together in a participatory and collaborative exercise known as "strategic planning". The general steps involved are usually these:

- Development of **Vision** and **Mission** statements

- Development of a **Values Statement**

- A list of **Goals and Objectives**

- A **SWOT Analysis** (review of strengths, weaknesses, opportunities and threats)

- A list of the resulting **Strategies and Tactics**

This type of planning work is usually carried out through facilitated sessions that may take a day or two to conduct. Some organizations will even do this as an off-site retreat. At the end of the process, written reports are drafted that will typically include a Strategic Plan and an Operating Plan (or Business Plan). The Strategic Plan might be a one-year plan or a multi-year plan. The Operating Plan is usually only for a one year period and is updated each year. These documents are critical in guiding the operations of the organization and formulating grant applications and other funding proposals.

Consultants that specialize in strategic planning work are

often hired to carry out this type of work since they have developed considerable expertise in best-practices methodology. A consultant will conduct background research into the organization and will design a cost-effective process that involves multiple stakeholders. Consultants will also bring considerable expert advice to the table because of their work with multiple organizations and work within the same sector. The consultant's role is a neutral third-party, which helps bring objectivity and fresh ideas to the process. The consultant will usually work with a small team including a facilitator and a note-taker. Their goal will be to facilitate consensus among stakeholders with differing points of view, to keep the planning committee on track, and to help organize all of the information gathered at the planning sessions into a cohesive strategic planning document.

Strategic planning consulting is great for people who like this kind of high-level thinking, are entrepreneurially-minded, and can manage stakeholders at a high level.

Facilitation & Training

It is often said that facilitation work is both a skill and an art. There are specific skills that a consultant must learn to become a facilitator, but it is also an art because the very best facilitators have a keen knack for the work—accompanied by the right personality and energy. Facilitators are hired for many different types of meetings where multiple stakeholders are brought together to work through a specific process. The facilitator will shape and guide the meeting so that the group meets its goals and works through the agenda or planning exercises effectively and on time. It might sound fairly simple, but it is actually quite an in-depth field and there is much to learn about facilitation. A facilitator's role involves a number of aspects such as:

- establishing meeting ground rules

- breaking the ice with creative exercises

- encouraging participation and ensuring all voices are heard

- guiding the group through a specific agenda (and staying on track)

- understanding the psychology of individuals and group dynamics

- understanding body language

- dealing with negativity and disruption

- gaining commitment

- bringing closure to items

- summarizing meeting results and establishing follow-up tasks

A good facilitator also has a strong sense of fun and is able to show a passionate commitment to the process. As well, effective public speaking skills are critical to maintaining group interest in the process. There is nothing worse than a day-long planning process with a boring and uncommitted facilitator. The very best facilitators inspire and excite a group toward action.

In this same category, I've also included training as a consulting specialty. Organizations often need to hire consultants who can, for example, train a group of door-to-door canvassers, train volunteers at a local food bank, or hold a board governance training session. Leadership and teaching skills, along with good oral communication skills are requirements to develop as a trainer.

Marketing & Communications

Opportunities abound for specializing as a marketing and communications consultant for nonprofits and charities. This can be a broad area that encompasses a number of different sub-specialty areas. Here are the most common organized into major categories:

Strategic & Tactical Planning:

- Marketing strategy development

- Campaign and tactical plan development

- Communications audits

- Policy and plan creation (social media plans, blog policies, communications guidelines)

Brand & Consumer Research:

- Brand perception studies

- Competitive and environmental assessments

- Brand development or revitalization

Tactical Channels:

- Digital (web, interactive, email, social media, mobile)

- Direct dialogue (door-to-door, street, malls, events)

- Direct mail

- Public relations and media

- Advertising buys

- Telemarketing

- Special events

- DRTV (Direct Response Television)

- Broadcast production management (radio, video)

Content Copywriting/Editing:

- Web content development

- Marketing collateral

- Newsletters

- Matte and blog articles (content marketing)

- Annual reports

- Program materials

Some marketing and communications consultants are generalists and can tackle the majority of these areas, but most specialize in one or two categories. For example, a strong marketing writer would easily manage any content development ranging from web content to print materials. That same person might also do PR work--drafting press releases and dealing with media. Another marketing consultant might focus on branding and strategy work as well as carrying out direct mail campaigns, telemarketing, and video production. There is a wide range of creative and interesting opportunities in the area of marketing, communications and publicity work.

Social Media Expert

Although social media work falls under the larger umbrella of marketing and communications, I've highlighted it as a unique subspecialty all its own. The need for expert social media support has exploded in the nonprofit sector, and many organizations are hiring full-time staff whose only job is managing social media channels. Many other organizations that cannot afford full-time help, will contract for part-time or virtual assistance on a regular basis. The other interesting element is that social media is always rapidly changing. Organizations look to the consulting experts for what's new, what's working, what's not and what's hot. It's easy to create a voice as an expert through maintaining an informative blog on this topic, developing useful resources, or speaking at conferences and workshops. Other work in this area can include developing social media guideline documents or offering staff training sessions on the business use of social media.

Project Management or Interim Management

If you are a generalist consultant, you can look for opportunities in discrete project management roles at a senior level such as overseeing large-scale events, major technology implementation projects, or large-scale team projects. Many organizations often require interim executive management when senior positions are vacant and going through a lengthy hiring process. If you don't mind working occasionally at a client site for set time periods, you can take a three to six month engagement. These kinds of roles also expose you to a variety of new skill areas and learning opportunities that boost your CV without a long-term commitment. You'll also have your foot in the door at a new organization with opportunities for continuing consulting work after your contract is complete.

Technology Consulting

Technology consulting can coexist within any of the areas of specialty being discussed here, but a focus in this area can also stand on its own with excellent consulting opportunities. Technology helps organizations function more efficiently and cheaply. Therefore, nonprofits and charities in particular, are keen to find new ways of building capacity through the use of technology. Being a technology consultant for nonprofits means that you understand the unique needs of the sector and know the best and most appropriate tools available to support their needs.

Examples of consulting in technology for nonprofits and charities includes the research, development and implementation of new technology systems in a number of possible areas:

- data audit and data assessments

- fundraising and donor assessments

- data hygiene, enhancements & transformation

- website development

- website content management

- Content Management Systems (CMS)

- Customer Relationship Management (CRM) solution

development and deployment

- database assessment, design and deployment

- permission-based email marketing applications

- campaign management and reporting systems

- technology training

If you have a background in technology and have had the opportunity to work for one or more nonprofit or charitable organizations, consider niching your tech skills in the voluntary sector. Nonprofits and charities have unique needs. Whenever these organizations source out supports and vendors, they prefer to work with companies who have direct experience in the nonprofit sector. Tap into conference and networking events specifically geared toward nonprofits and charities in order to get a better sense of what this means. One of the premier organizations in this arena is the Nonprofit Technology Network based in the US. See the following resources section for more information.

Technology Resources

Nonprofit Technology Network: www.nten.org
NTEN is the premier tech resource based in the US. The description from the NTEN website at nten.org says it best:

"NTEN aspires to a world where all nonprofit organizations use technology skillfully and confidently to meet community needs and fulfill their missions. We are the membership organization of nonprofit technology professionals. Our members share the common goal of helping nonprofits use all aspects of technology more effectively. We believe that technology allows nonprofits to work with greater social impact. We enable our members to strategically use technology to make the world a better, just, and equitable place. NTEN facilitates the exchange of knowledge and information within our community. We connect our members to each other, provide professional development opportunities, educate our constituency on issues of technology use in nonprofits, and spearhead groundbreaking research, advocacy, and education on technology issues affecting our entire community."

This is a perfect description of the potential role that consultants can play in the technology arena. NTEN offers membership, networking, training, and a fantastic annual conference that you won't want to miss if this area of consulting interests you.

TechSoup Canada and TechSoup Global: www.techsoupcanada.ca, www.techsoup.org
Another excellent technology resource is TechSoup which

has both a US and Canadian branch. The Canadian site is at techsoupcanada.ca. Techsoup is a nonprofit technology assistance agency that establishes strategic partnerships with major technology companies like Microsoft, Symantec, Adobe and Cisco, to provide discounted software and other resources to nonprofit organizations. They also offer online training, networking forums, and other great resources so be sure to check them out.

CHAPTER SEVEN

From Cubicle to Consulting: Making the Transition

Okay so not everyone is stuck with the dreaded cubicle from Monday to Friday, but chances are, if you are reading this book, you just might be--and I'll bet you are itching to get out. But how do I get started, you wonder? How do I deal with having bills to pay and relying on that regular paycheque? How do I transition from the security of a full-time 9 to 5 job to a home-based consulting business?

Obviously, it's going to be different for everyone—for some it might be quite easy, but for others more of a challenge. I'm going to give you a few ideas and strategies to make the transition and build a consulting practice. The main thing is that you must have a strong drive to do this. You will need to test drive that important skill I already described as a critical requirement of consulting work—self-discipline. You will need to make some sacrifices and be willing to change your usual routine. But if you've made it this far and you think you have what it takes, then it is time to make a solid plan and the right adjustments to reach your new goal. There are two key stumbling blocks that you need to work through—one is time and the other is money.

Finding the Time

If you have lots of time on your hands to explore a new career—time for training, going to seminars, doing the marketing work involved—then you can probably skip this chapter and dive right in. Good for you because changing careers requires a significant time commitment in order to focus on your new business. However, I'm going to assume that you are in a full time job at present, and that you have very little time to devote to making a career change in the first place, other than knowing that you want a change and need to quit the rat race. Here are a few ideas that might help you consider how to deal with having a lack of time:

- Temporarily change jobs to a less demanding time commitment and work environment—one that is either part time or nightshift work where you can spend some time during the day or a couple of days a week focusing on your new career.

- Consider altering your existing job to a condensed 4-day work week or part-time role. Some organizations offer work-life balance programs for those times when people have personal demands such as raising kids or caring for a sick family member. You may have to come up with a viable reason for the change since obviously you can't tell your employer that you're starting a new business. Perhaps you have a difficult commute or a health issue that you can use to make a business case for a 4-day work week.

- Free up your schedule on the weekends and dedicate Saturday or Sunday – or even a half day to focusing on your new career.

- Dedicate an hour or two each evening at least a couple of times a week to working on your new career.

The idea here is that you need to somehow free up a block of dedicated time during your week to focus on your new goals. If you can carve out one full day or even a half day, you can get a lot accomplished. In fact, you will be quite surprised as just a few weeks go by, how having that dedicated time available to you will make a big difference in launching your new career. Eliminate all distractions during that day—don't answer emails or do anything else—just focus on your home-based business. Not only will you be working toward your goal, but you will find that this time energizes and excites you. You'll like forward to this time each week. A new horizon will begin to open up and changes will start to happen in multiple ways in your life—from how you handle your money, decisions you make at work, and tasks or other plans you choose to take on for the next few months.

Financial Concerns

Your second biggest challenge to launching a new career is likely going to be financial. For at least the first year and possibly longer, your annual salary may take a nosedive. There's a saying that the more we make, the more we spend, so my advice to you in order to make this work and to meet your long term goals, is to get a good grip on your finances right now. Here's some ways you can do that:

- Sit down and create an annual budget for yourself to figure out how much money you need to live on each month.

- Scale back on all discretionary spending and put yourself on a serious spending freeze. Cancel magazine subscriptions, increase deductibles on insurance, stop buying Starbucks lattes, eat at home— do whatever you can to cut back your spending.

- If you can qualify, apply for a line of credit (secured or unsecured) with the same bank where you have your chequing account and link it online so that borrowing and paying back is very easy. Tap into this account only when you need to and pay it off as quickly as possible.

- If you're still in the planning stages and working full-time, start putting aside some money each month in a savings account that you can use to have some safety funds for when you launch your business.

- Let family and friends know that you are undertaking a career change so that you set expectations for socializing or gift giving.

- Put a moratorium on shopping for at least 6 months and make do with your current wardrobe.

Once you make this kind of tough financial assessment, you might actually be surprised how little you really need to pay your fixed bills each month. Just remember to stay focused on your goals to stay motivated. If necessary, write out what you want to achieve over the next couple of years and post it in a prominent place. Some people like to create vision boards so that ideas and dreams are illustrated in picture form.

When I made the transition from the 9-to-5 world to

working for myself, it took me about three years in total. At the beginning, I was working for a large management consulting firm on Bay Street in Toronto. I had about 15 years of solid administrative and management work experience by this time and had recently been headhunted into this particular role where I was managing administrative services at seven offices across the country. I had about 50 administrative staff reporting in to me and my salary was just under six figures. Sounds like a dream job that most people would kill for, but within about six months I was hating it. I was bored out of my mind in meetings. Doing tasks that I dreaded. I literally dragged myself to work every day. I knew that I wanted to do something much more interesting, more fulfilling and less stressful.

The problem was that I was a single mom with two young children and a mortgage to pay. My job was also extremely demanding and I had no time to think about how to get out of this situation. I remember at the time, confiding in my dad and telling him that I was unhappy with my new job. He suggested that I think about a time when I had a job that made me just enough money to pay the bills, but didn't consume me. If I found a job like that and could get by with it, I would then have the time and energy to focus on what to do next. It was great advice because a light bulb went off in my head. I remembered a job I had years prior where I worked as a word processor in a secretarial pool at a large law firm. The money was decent and it was brainless work.

So that's literally what I did. I sent out ten resumes to the ten largest law firms in downtown Toronto that I knew had word-processing centres. I had to dumb down my resume quite a bit, but I was so overqualified that I got three job offers within about a month. I picked the best paying one with the right scheduling flexibility and gave notice at my current job. It was funny at the time because the law firm was just around the corner from my management job. The word-processing job turned out to be perfect for what I needed for my transition period. It paid pretty well, there were day and evening shifts to choose from, I could work as much or as little as I wanted to from week to week, and most important of all—it was mindless work. My brain had lots of energy left over to focus on crafting my new future career.

The Transition Phase

Once you've laid the foundation for your transition into consultancy, you can start looking for small contracts that you can easily manage. This is useful whether you have a full-time job or not because it will help you gain confidence that you can work for yourself and are capable of making money as a consultant. Tell everyone you know about your new venture. Approach organizations that interest you and ask about their work needs. Perhaps you can write a grant for a local choir or pitch improvements to a website for a neighbourhood charitable group. You might do it for a low fee which is a win-win for both parties. You'll get the work experience and they'll get some inexpensive support.

Eventually, there will be a point where you'll need to free up even more time. Ideally, you'll need at least half of your week in order to be able to take on any real consulting assignments. One of the best ways to manage this, while still paying your bills, is to start scanning job boards for a part time, regular job with a nonprofit or charity. This could be permanent part time or a time-limited contract role. A part time regular job will give you some stability as you build up your client work. It will also free up more time during the week to develop your business.

Once you identify a job opportunity and get selected for a job offer, try to maintain as much control as you can over the work situation in two ways:

1. **Work at Home**. Does the job require that you be present at the office location of this client? During the interview process, explore whether they are open to a virtual work arrangement either all of the time or part of the time. Market yourself as a "freelance consultant" from the start and explain that you have a fully equipped home office. If they are not open to this, then at this stage you can't be too choosey, so take the job anyway—especially if it's a good opportunity.

2. **Get Paid as a Consultant**. Explore with the client whether you would be paid as a payroll employee or as a freelance consultant. It may or may not make sense depending on the type of work you'll be doing, but it will always be to your advantage to be paid as a consultant. Be sure you understand any taxation rules around consultants versus employees before making this pitch to the client. See the next section for more information on this distinction.

The reason for negotiating the above two areas in your favour, is that you want to start living, working, and acting like a consultant as soon as you can. You need to move away from the model and mindset of an "employee" and become more independent and more entrepreneurial. There are also financial and tax advantages to being paid as a consultant. For example, if a salaried job involves more than 20 hours a week, the employer is required to pay benefits and vacation pay. These benefits can be worth up to 15% of the cost of a salary. As a consultant, you are better off putting that money in your pocket, so you can often negotiate for a higher hourly rate. As a consultant working out of a home office, you'll also benefit from home office tax deductions, which don't apply if you are a salaried employee.

With your first part time regular "client" in place, you are ready to really launch your new consulting practice. You should now have at least two days a week that you can devote to the business side of things—marketing, networking, skill development, and writing proposals for new work. We'll cover all these areas in detail in subsequent chapters. I just want you to understand the best way to make this transitional period work with the least amount of disruption to your finances or personal life. Over time, it's ideal if you can keep one good paying, part-time regular client on your client list. While transitioning, you cannot be too particular, but eventually you'll be able to maintain the client work that gives you the most satisfaction, the best work-life balance lifestyle, and a rate of pay that you feel you are worth. You'll accomplish this by slowing dropping off the clients that don't meet this criteria and hanging on to the ones that do.

After settling into my new job in the law firm word processing centre, I started working on my strategy to transition back into the voluntary sector. I had only one job in the sector—working for a number of years at The Law Society of Upper Canada—but I also had a lot of volunteer and community exposure. I knew I had to structure my resume in such a way as to draw on the cross-functional skills I had rather than a traditional job list resume. I'll show you how to do that in the following chapter. My salary took a big hit with this job change, and was only a little more than half what it was before. I had a tight budget and literally could not spend a dollar on anything extra that was not in my budget.

After about seven months at the law firm, I was successful in landing a full time job as Operations Manager for the Canadian Children's Opera Chorus. It was truly my dream job since I loved working with children, I am an amateur musician myself, and it would give me my needed foray back into the voluntary sector. Unfortunately, the honeymoon was short lived and I only survived about nine months on this job. The role was typical of a lot of smaller charities in that a monumental amount of work was heaped into a single job description. For various reasons, including my struggle to manage raising two young kids as a single mother, I came to the difficult decision that the job fit was not right so I left the role. However, while I was there, I was exposed to multiple new skill areas unique to voluntary sector work: grant writing, grant reporting, grant tracking, corporate and foundation proposals and asks, volunteer management, fundraising and gala event management, marketing and PR, music CD production, web site development, and more.

For the first time in my working years, I found myself unemployed—a pretty scary predicament for a single mother with a mortgage to pay. It was at this point that I knew I simply had to start working for myself. I just couldn't go back to a 9-to-5 daily grind. I needed work-life balance and I wanted to be available for my kids—to be home to cook healthy meals, and to have much less stress in my life. I felt that I had gained enough experience to launch a freelance business. I had also just cut back drastically on my overhead spending so it was now or never.

So rather than search for another full-time job, I started looking for part-time roles in the voluntary sector. I felt focused and confident that I had found the type of work that made me happy. I had always been heavily involved in my community doing volunteer work ranging from food co-operatives, to community pre-teen dances, to local fundraisers. I was also really good at this sort of work. All of the business experience I had gained in the for-profit sector equipped me to bring value to the administration and viability of these types of community ventures.

Within about six weeks, I found and was hired for a role working with an entrepreneurial medical doctor who was working on return to work initiatives. The doctor had a home-based office and I worked with her in her home office two days a week with additional hours spent working out of my own home office. In total, I was billing about 20 hours a week as a freelance consultant. The work I did involved a number of areas including business strategy, government grant proposals, grant reporting, and presentation development.

This regular weekly gig paid the bills and when I wasn't working on this billable work, I started developing my website and focusing my business goals. I slowly began attracting other work here and there—mostly grant writing and foundation proposal letters. To fill the rest of my week, I did some volunteer work for a Toronto-based arts foundation and at the Royal Ontario Museum. I went to seminars and conferences, and I joined the Toronto chapter of the Association of Fundraising Professionals. I wasn't raking in a high salary, but I had never been happier. Best of all, I was home when my kids got home from school and there when they needed me.

Over the next few years, I finished my assignment with the doctor and acquired new clients including the Association in Defence of the Wrongly Convicted, Pro Bono Law Ontario, and Christian Children's Fund of Canada, to name a few. I always maintained at least one regular weekly client so that I had a foundation of billable hours. At various times, I also worked with other consultants who had larger consulting practices than my own. They had overflow work which they outsourced to me and other consultants.

Employee Versus Contractor

It's important to understand the distinction between an Employee—which is an employee-employer relationship and an Independent Consultant—which is a business relationship. The reason for the difference is that employees are put on a payroll and the employer pays for things like benefits, vacation pay, employment insurance and government pension amounts. Consultants on the other hand, must pay for their own employment insurance or pension amounts, don't receive benefits or vacation pay from the employer, and can deduct their own business expenses. As mentioned in this chapter, you want to be treated as a **Consultant** since the income, tax and career advantages are greater for you with this arrangement.

This is the general criteria that Canada Revenue would

consider if the work arrangement was ever put in question:

1. **Degree of Autonomy or Control.** A Consultant is assigned a work deliverable and exercises a large amount of control over how the work is carried out. In other words, the Consultant works independently within a defined framework. A Consultant does not have anyone overseeing their day-to-day activities. They are free to choose their work hours and to provide services to multiple clients.

2. **Tools and Equipment.** A Consultant makes an investment in the tools and equipment needed to carry out their work in addition to paying for the cost of maintaining that equipment. A Consultant also supplies their own workspace and pays for the cost of that space.

3. **Financial Risk & Opportunity for Profit.** A Consultant takes on both a financial risk and increased opportunity for profit than an Employee.

4. **Investment & Management.** A Consultant may choose to sub-contract some or all of the work they have been hired to do. They are compensated based on a flat service or hourly fee and may have to invest additional costs in performing the services.

For more detail on the above, visit the Canada Revenue Agency website at www.cra-arc.gc.ca and search for the publication called "Employee or self-employed?"

In the United States, the test is similar and is based on common-law rules. From www.irs.gov *Independent*

Contractor (Self-employed) or Employee?

Facts that provide evidence of the degree of control and independence fall into three categories:

1. **Behavioral:** Does the company control or have the right to control what the worker does and how the worker does his or her job?

2. **Financial:** Are the business aspects of the worker's job controlled by the payer? (these include things like how worker is paid, whether expenses are reimbursed, who provides tools/supplies, etc.)

3. **Type of Relationship:** Are there written contracts or employee type benefits (i.e. pension plan, insurance, vacation pay, etc.)? Will the relationship continue and is the work performed a key aspect of the business?

If you live in another country, check your government's taxation information so you understand what the rules are around working as an independent contractor, taxation, and tax deductions.

CHAPTER EIGHT
Converting Your Resume to a CV

As a consultant, you will need to sell yourself based on your past skills and experience. You'll do this through written proposals and in person meetings. One of the foundational documents in your proposals will be your Curriculum Vitae— or "CV" for short. A CV is like a resume, but a more professional version of a resume. To create one, you will need to convert your traditional resume into a CV. While a resume is normally a brief one-page chronological list of education and work experience, a CV is a longer, more detailed description of your skills, experience, training and any other relevant details. The benefit of the CV for a consultant is that it gives a much clearer picture of the work you are capable of doing and it downplays details that might not work in your favour such as how long you were at a job or what your job title was. There are many different ways to draft a CV depending on the profession since they are more commonly used for academic and research positions. However, I will show you a format that works really well for consulting.

Before drafting a CV, your first step is to create an inventory of personal information under the main categories listed below. Save this inventory as a separate document and keep it updated so that you always have a master reference file to use for drafting and updating your CV. You might only need a single CV—especially if you are specializing in one area of consultancy. However, if you are more of a generalist, you will need to tailor your CV each time you target a new client.

Skills & Experience Inventory

Highlighted Skills
Make a list of your high-level skill areas or core competencies. When you draft your CV, you will list three to six of these at the very top of the first page. These skill areas will stand out to the reader at a glance. They can be a list of your main consulting areas or they can be deeper core competencies. Use just one to two-word phrases to describe these core competencies.

Consulting Areas
Make a list of about three or four consulting areas or sub-areas that you seek to provide service in. Under each area, list all of the things that you have done in the past in this area or are capable of doing.

Professional Experience (Client Assignments)
Maintain an ongoing inventory of your client assignments here. If you are just starting out, list your past work experience and job titles.

Key Achievements
Note any key achievements you may have accomplished in a

professional setting. These should relate to significant outcomes such as generating new business streams or achieving high financial or other targets for a client.

Education
List your formal education here, school(s) attended, and any degrees received.

Professional Training & Development
Create and then keep an ongoing list of all the training and professional development opportunities you participate in.

Publications
List any written work you have done including published books or articles.

Memberships/Affiliations
List any memberships or affiliations that you keep.

Community/Volunteer Experience
List volunteer experience. Keep track of the organization or group, what your role was, and the time period (year to year).

Once you have a robust inventory in these categories, draft a brief paragraph that summarizes your professional profile that you will use as an "Introduction" or "Executive Profile." This summary will be the opening section of your CV.

It's difficult to tell you exactly how to write your own CV

because every person's will be different. You may only use some of the categories above or you may find all of them useful. See the end of this chapter for a sample that might help you get started. Here's a few other tips to keep in mind:

- Unlike a resume, a CV can be as many pages as needed. The sample I've included is just one page and normally would be more detailed. However, still aim to keep your writing succinct and clearly written. If necessary, use headings such as "Selected Assignments" or "Selected Publications" if you have a large volume of experience. Choose the top 6 or 7 items that best fit with the client sector you are pitching.

- Make absolutely sure your CV is proofread multiple times so that it is free of grammatical errors and typos.

- Avoid the use of the "I" pronoun in your text—instead, use bullet points starting with positive action words such as "initiated," "created," "managed," as some examples.

- Avoid acronyms that the reader might not understand, however be sure to use any language or buzzwords relevant to your area of specialization.

- Don't use coloured stationery or unusual fonts. Keep it simple and stick with basic fonts such as Times, Arial, Helvetica, Verdana, or Century Gothic.

- Leave out references unless you are specifically asked for them.

- Do not include irrelevant details such as marital status, gender, or children.

- Start your CV with your name and contact information. Do not include the title "CV" or "Resume" at the top. The reader will know that the document is a CV so the title is redundant.

Ellen Jones

ellenjones@gmail.com
www.ellenconsulting.com
555-222-1234

Executive Profile

A seasoned professional with diverse marketing, communications, and public relations experience. Strong creative, strategic, and collaborative team-builder. Proven experience developing traditional and digital communications strategies across multi-channel platforms. Adept at consumer, donor and stakeholder engagement.

Core Competencies

- **Brand Innovation**
- **Communications Planning**
- **Project Management**

Marketing & Communications

Writing, production, and management of marketing and communications deliverables in both for-profit and nonprofit/charity environments including brand and content development, revenue development, web content management, collateral materials development, and public relations activities.

Facilitation & Planning

Skilled facilitator bringing creativity and insight to small or large group learning processes. Strong experience in strategic planning, with well-developed relational, communication and project management skills. Skilled in analysis and strategy relating to complex systems.

Project Management
Diverse leadership experience in project management. Experience analyzing business and funding requirements for organizations, conducting environmental scans, communications audits, literature reviews, and other types of trend and issue analyses to inform business goals. Strong commitment to working with shared leadership and in cross-functional teams.

Professional Experience/Recent Clients
World Vision
Greenpeace
University of Toronto
Brookfield Children's Hospital

Education
University of Toronto, Canada - Bachelor of Arts - Business
College of Applied Arts & Technology, Canada - Post-Graduate Certification in Media Relations

Memberships & Affiliations
Canadian Marketing Association
Association of Fundraising Professionals

Volunteer Experience
Sunnybrook Hospital Foundation - Member of Board of Directors, 2015 - 2016
Humane Society - Volunteer, 2008 - 2015

CHAPTER NINE
Where to Find Work

The steps involved in finding work as a consultant are similar to the tasks and strategy of any salesperson. You need to constantly be on the lookout—networking and marketing yourself in small and large ways. Salespeople refer to the process of generating business leads as "filling the funnel." Even when you are busy with work and booked at full capacity, you should keep up activities that will provide you with future work opportunities down the road. The idea is to eliminate as much down time as possible in between client assignments.

Generally speaking, there are three ways to find consulting work:

1. Searching Job Boards

2. Networking

3. Outreach & Marketing

I'm going to focus primarily on job board resources in this chapter. In the next chapter, I'll talk about outreach and marketing. In regards to networking, this is something you should start doing now and continue to do on an ongoing basis. If you already have some connections with community agencies, nonprofit groups, or even charities, connect with your network as soon as possible and let them know that you are launching a consulting practice. Make it a habit to schedule at least one lunch every month with someone from your network including friends, colleagues and past clients. Take a sincere interest in what's happening with previous clients and let them know what work you've been involved with. You never know when a project will come up and you want to be sure they think of you first. Friends and colleagues often have connections to organizations that you might be unaware of. Keep them informed on your new career and stay attuned to new networks they might introduce you to. Do this constantly both in person and through social media channels.

One of the best ways to find new business is to be constantly scouring nonprofit and charity job boards. This is easy to do since these resources have online systems for sending automatic searches right to your in-box. When you launch your new business, you should register on these sites and set up relevant searches. I've listed some of the top resources in the United States and Canada. Note that my instructions for these are accurate at time of writing, but if the site has changed format, you'll just need to figure out how to set up a search. If you are in another country, a simple Google search will help you locate the best job boards. Remember too that as a consultant you can work globally if the work is virtual, so don't neglect to check out multiple market areas.

When setting up searches, choose categories such as Part Time, Contract, Parental/Maternity Leave, in addition to

RFP (Request for Proposal), RFI (Request for Information) and RFX (Request for Information). Different sites may use different terminology.

If you find other good online resources with job boards or postings that do not have an auto-email system, here is what you can do. Set up a bookmark folder and bookmark the site in that folder. Approximately once a month, visit each site to check for any new postings.

Online Job and RFP (Tender) Boards

Canadian Resources:

Charity Village: www.charityvillage.com
Charity Village is one of the foremost online resources in Canada where the majority of nonprofits and charities post their job openings. Visit the site and register for a free account. Next, navigate to the Job Search section, click on Advanced Search, select your region and then multi-select "Contract-Part Time," "Part Time" and "Parental Leave Coverage-Part Time". Leave the other choices open so you have a nice wide search and can see what's out there. You can always refine this at a later date. Click on the "Search" button at the bottom to get your results page. Then choose "Save Search" and a pop-up box will open. From here, give your search a name and at the bottom of this box you will see a checkbox for "Email Results Daily." Make sure this is checked off. Next, set up a second search on "Request for Proposal," but for this one, make the search Canada wide. Many consulting jobs can be handled virtually so make this a broader search. If you're transitioning into your new business, Charity Village is the best place to look for regular part time gigs. Be patient; these part-time jobs don't come out all the time, but you should see at least a couple each month.

MERX: www.merx.com
MERX is an online database of tender opportunities posted by government departments, Crown and other agencies across Canada. There are two subscription levels to choose from—one is a pay-as-you-go system and the other is around

$200 a year for unlimited access to all postings. You can even subscribe further to access tenders out of the U.S. Once registered, log onto the system and set up an Opportunity Matching Profile, which is essentially an automated search that emails you with any matches. With a basic subscription, you are allowed one free profile or can pay a nominal monthly fee for additional profiles. To understand how to set up your profile, watch the tutorial video on the site. Then use whatever keywords fit your area of interest.

Ontario Tenders Portal: www.ontariotenders.bravosolutions.com

In 2014, the Ontario government changed their electronic tendering system from Merx to BravoSolutions. Register on the site as a supplier and search for open RFI (Request for Information) and RFX (Request for Information, Quote, or Proposal) opportunities relevant to your consulting practice.

Work in Nonprofits: www.workinnonprofits.ca

Work in Nonprofits is a small job board, which might show duplication of jobs posted on Charity Village, but it can't hurt to set up a job alert here. Sign up and then set up your search choosing Part time, Contract-Part time, and Request for Proposal for your region or Canada-wide.

Arts & Culture Job Boards

Work In Culture (Ontario): www.workinculture.ca/The-Job-Board
Alliance for Arts & Culture (British Columbia): www.allianceforarts.com/job-board

Work in Culture and the Alliance for Arts & Culture are two

good sites with job boards that support the arts and culture sector. There are a few smaller sites for other areas across Canada, but many jobs are cross-posted on Charity Village. However, it can't hurt to check these sites out occasionally. Unfortunately, neither has an auto-email function so you have to remind yourself once a month or so to take a look. There aren't too many RFP postings here, so you would mainly be looking for part-time or contract assignments. Both sites let you filter the search based on "part time" as a search term.

Workopolis: Workopolis.ca – nonprofit and charity sections

Again, most nonprofits and charities will use Charity Village, but it can't hurt to set up an alert on Workopolis. After registering, select "Part Time" and "Not-for-profit and Charity" industry.

Association of Fundraising Professionals: www.afpnet.org plus local chapters

If fundraising is your area of specialization, then it's critical to become a member of your local chapter of the Association of Fundraising Professionals. The AFP is a global organization with about 30,000 members worldwide. The job board within each local chapter has postings that will not necessarily appear on Charity Village and other sites so be sure to check here for opportunities or better yet, become a member of AFP because there are lots of great reasons for joining.

U.S. Resources:

Idealist: www.idealist.org
Idealist is a nonprofit clearinghouse with a robust jobs
board. Click on the jobs link and choose Temporary, Part
Time and Contract. Then click on the link to set up an Email
Alert. Idealist also has a volunteer resource section that can
help you find volunteer opportunities that can lead to regular
work.

Monster: www.Monster.com
Monster is one of the large job sites which also has a
charitable section so it might be worthing setting a search up
here.

North American Resources:

Fresh Gigs: www.freshgigs.ca
Fresh Gigs is a national site that targets both non-profit and
for-profit jobs primarily for marketing, communications, and
creative work. This site does have an auto-email function so
register on the site and set up a search using the filter
"freelance".

Elance: www.elance.com
Elance is an online global site for freelancers of all kinds. The
way the site works is that you create a profile and you bid for
work along with other freelancers. I personally haven't had
much luck with this site in the past, but you can find some
local organizations using it. I found that a lot of the work was
small in time and scope, which makes it a lot of work to go
through the proposal process.

LinkedIn: www.linkedin.com
It's critical that you have an updated and fully completed profile on LinkedIn. Be sure to connect with all of your friends, past colleagues, and past clients on an ongoing basis. Join relevant groups and follow some of the top organizations in the nonprofit world including fundraising groups, marketing associations, technology associations or any relevant groups and associations. Once you've done that, check out the job search tools available on LinkedIn to source out any potential leads for client work. The search feature is not very robust unless you have a Premium subscription.

Craigslist: www.craigslist.org
Depending on where you live, Craigslist can sometimes provide some interesting leads. Visit the jobs section and select part-time and non-profit to see what's available. You'll have to wade through a lot of ads for restaurant servers and "earn extra income!" ads, but you never know what you might find. Also check out sections such as "writer/editor" and "nonprofit sector" for additional postings.

CHAPTER TEN
Marketing You & Your Business

If you don't know much about marketing, consider hiring an expert to help you develop a marketing plan. There are lots of different tactics to choose from in marketing a business, but I'm going to focus on the areas where I believe you will be most effective with the least amount of effort. Online marketing is key, but direct networking and outreach are also important.

Online Marketing – Web Site

A few short years ago, I may have told you that having a website was optional, but today that's no longer the case. Every organization you work with will have an online presence. They will use technology in different ways and they will no doubt be using social media. As a consultant, it's essential to act as a role model when it comes to use of technology. You don't have to be an expert, but you should at least show that you understand the basics. If you don't have a website and a LinkedIn profile at a bare minimum, how can a client expect you to understand the importance of technology to business processes? Another advantage of having a website is that it acts as your online business card and helps when you are pitching new business. Whether people find you online, or whether you answer an RFP and people look you up online, a clear and descriptive website is important for you to have.

One of the easiest and cheapest ways to set up a website within a matter of minutes is to use Wordpress.com. Wordpress started as an online blogging tool and is still essentially a blogging system, but over the past several years, many people starting using a free Wordpress account to create a website. I'm going to tell you the basics of how to do this, but you can also find lots of information and tips online to get more elaborate with this system. You can either set up a static website on Wordpress, but one of the benefits of the system is to also use it for blogging. Blogging is a great way to show your subject matter expertise, but it is also beneficial for creating positive search engine optimization.

If creating your own website is too onerous for you or you simply do not have the time or inclination to tackle it DIY, you can easily find local web developers to set up a simple site for you. Expect to pay around $2,000 to $5,000 depending on the level of customization.

Here are the basic steps for creating a website using Wordpress:

1. Visit www.wordpress.com and register for either a free or premium account.

2. A free blog address will have the name sitename.wordpress.com. You can start with this address for now and then later on if you register your own domain name, you can change this setting within Wordpress so that your site is directed to that new

URL address. Alternatively, upon sign-up, you can purchase a domain name directly through Wordpress.

3. Once you are all set up and logged in, you will be able to access the Dashboard of your site. Down the left side of the screen, you will find all of the different areas for setting up and customizing your site. Click on the site name next to the globe in the upper left corner and you can toggle back and forth between the Dashboard and the online view of your site. Click around in the Dashboard choices to begin to understand how the system works.

4. At this point, your website will be in the default setting which means that the homepage or first page of the site is a blog page. You can either leave it this way if you plan to write some articles and do a little blogging, or you can turn the Home Page into a static page and make your site look more like a traditional website. To do that, follow these instructions: https://en.support.wordpress.com/pages/front-page/

5. Once you have the blog versus static site issue settled, you can begin creating other pages that you would like to have, such as About, Services, Clients and a Contact page.

6. The next step is to give your site a bit of pizzazz by changing the theme. Theme is the visual design and layout of a Wordpress site. When you first set up your account, the theme will be a basic default theme, but you can change this by going into the Dashboard and choosing Appearance—Themes. Many of the themes available are free, but some are considered Premium

themes which have a one-time cost to purchase. You might want to start with a free theme and get your site set up before spending money on a premium theme. You can preview different options by clicking on the Preview button. Keep in mind though that many of the themes require you to upload a header image or to do a bit of additional set-up. You won't get a full idea of how the theme looks unless you activate it. Once you find something you like, click on Activate and return to your Dashboard. Next, click on the different options under Appearance to manage other customization options.

By now you are either pulling your hair out or happily patting yourself on the back for designing your own website. If you are the former, hopefully you can find a tech-savvy relative or friend to help you get started. For more resources and tutorials, visit http://learn.wordpress.com

Online Marketing – Social Media

Whether you choose to have a website or not, you definitely **must** set up or update your LinkedIn profile. LinkedIn has withstood some tough competition among social media channels and stands out as the number one professional online networking system of the day. If you'd like to also have a Facebook business page and/or a Twitter account, set those up as well. If you are going to blog from your website, set up your Wordpress site to autopost to your social media sites every time you create a blogpost.

Personal Branding & Content Marketing

Over the past few years, there's been tremendous growth

around the concept of personal branding. Personal branding is all about people marketing their image and careers as brands. It's a way of defining yourself as a leader and subject matter expert in your field. By focusing on developing your personal brand, you can leverage this as a terrific marketing tool. Your website is most definitely the place to start. Blogging is the perfect outreach mechanism for content marketing. Sharing knowledge, your personal perspective on different issues, and illustrating your leadership skills in a particular area is a great way to attract potential new clients. If you enjoy blogging and using social media, you can begin to develop a following and add people to an electronic mailing list. Autopost your articles to a Facebook page and to Twitter. Post updates and articles on LinkedIn. Engage with people who follow you to create a dialogue. Join LinkedIn groups and start conversations.

If your message clicks with people and you start to develop a sizeable following, consider launching an electronic newsletter. This is a powerful outreach tool—especially if you build your business to include a team of employees. Repurpose your blog posts or curate content from other resources, add in some visuals, and send it out to your blog followers once a month. Include icons for people to share your newsletter, like your Facebook page, or connect in other ways.

In your email software, find the feature for email signatures and create a professional signature using a different font from your email text and a bit of colour. Include your web address, email and phone. You can also include links or icon links to your social media pages.

If you feel that you've developed a particular expertise and you like to write, convert some of your blog posts into longer articles and submit to sites like Charity Village and Idealist.

Another effective outreach tactic is speaking at conventions and seminars where you can lead small workshops on topics of interest to nonprofits and charities. These can be held in person or online as a webinar. You always want to make these sessions about providing value and not to be overtly selling yourself. By crafting your message and the information you provide, you can leave an audience feeling that you have much more value to offer if they hire you. Speaking and consulting are fully interrelated. I can guarantee at the end of any session, you will have people come up to you and ask for your business card. If you publish an electronic newsletter, put out a sign-up list to capture new prospect leads.

Eventually you might build your knowledge to the point that you can stand out as a thought leader in your particular area. If you are a skilled facilitator and speaker you can get paid for speaking at large scale events or leading training and workshops. Other possible income streams are leadership programs, coaching, books and e-books or online training programs.

Networking and Direct Marketing

Once you have your website established, another way to reach out to potential organizations, is to target them directly. Start creating a mailing list of organizations that interest you. Or, view job postings and email the personnel contact directly. Mention that you are a consultant, describe your area of expertise, and pitch your services. Create a couple of different email templates that you can copy/paste from and send these emails out on a daily basis. A company might be searching for a full time employee, but take interest in an interim consultant or outsourcing critical projects while they conduct their job search.

Leverage Your Client Portfolio

As you start to get client work, be sure to use your current work to build upon future work. Two important marketing tools are testimonials and work samples. Anytime you complete a client assignment, ask your client for a written testimonial. Sometimes these will come to you unsolicited since clients will often send a parting card with words of thanks. But remember to ask the client while your work is fresh on their minds. Post your testimonials to your website. Sincere reflections like this from past clients are powerful. Having work samples are important to future proposals, but you can also describe some examples of your work on your website. If you do any sort of visual work such as websites or marketing materials, post image samples on a client work page to illustrate the kind of projects you have been involved with. Create small thumbnail images and link those to larger pdf files. Be careful though about posting any confidential client information. If you provide client work as samples in your proposals, you may need to redact any names or sensitive information.

Taking the above a step further, considering incorporating the concept of **value-based marketing** in your outreach efforts. Value-based marketing means providing something of value to potential clients. Think about any tools you might have developed in the course of your consulting work that other nonprofit and charitable organizations might find useful. This could be a work process flowchart, critical path to strategic planning, position papers on various topics —to name a few ideas. Post these on your website as free downloads. Just make sure you are the author of these tools or have substantially modified other resources to make it your own original work. You can also incorporate a lead generation form to collect a user's name and email before they receive the download. Follow up with this lead to see if you can assist them in some way. Add the lead to your mailing list database.

CHAPTER ELEVEN
Setting Up Your Business

So I hope by now you can officially announce that you are a small business owner! As soon as you can make the announcement, be sure you understand all the registration and taxation rules in your area. Most countries allow for an informal establishment of a business sole proprietorship. For new consultants, I suggest that you keep things simple to start with. If your business grows to include hiring staff or has income and assets beyond $150,000 a year, at that point you can consider more complex business structures such as partnerships or incorporation.

Government & Tax Business Registration

If you want to begin working as a freelancer, you can do that under your own name and operate as an individual—billing clients using your name. This is the simplest kind of business structure to use. In North America, the legal structure for this setup is known as a *sole proprietorship*. A sole proprietorship is an unincorporated business owned by a single individual. You can set up your sole proprietorship using your own name or a business name. If you choose to use a business name, you will need to register that name with the government. The reason for this is to make sure you are not choosing a name that some other business is using. In Canada, the business registration process is managed federally and can be done online. Visit Canada Revenue Service's Business Registration Online for more details. In the US, business registration is handled at the state level Requirements vary depending on which state you live in. The process is called *Doing Business As* or DBA for short. For example, Google "DBA in New York State" using whatever state you are in for the search term.

The next step is to determine whether you need to collect sales tax on your services. In Canada, sales tax is charged on consulting services once you make more than $30,000 annually before expenses, although you can also choose to collect tax from day one of your new business. In the US, again it varies by state and depends upon the type of consulting services you provide. Google information on state tax for your particular state so you understand exactly what's involved right from the start. If you are serious about launching your career as a consultant, I would recommend that you choose a specific business start date, properly register your business, and begin collecting sales tax on any work that you do. In fact, as soon as you begin setting up your business—purchasing a new laptop, buying a new desk, supplies or anything else you need, you can use those costs as legitimate business expenses. Save your receipts and when you file your annual federal tax return, take advantage of these early home office business expenses. If you only make a small amount consulting in your first year—say $5,000— your legitimate business expenses might result in a loss. You can then use this loss to offset any salaried income you still have. You can show a loss for a couple of years if necessary.

Anything beyond that might raise a flag with Canada Revenue or the Internal Revenue Service, but a year or two of losses for a new business is not unusual.

When setting up your business registration, beware that there are many third-party online companies that claim to offer business registration services for a fee. I would recommend that you stick with the legitimate government sites. This is cheaper and it is very easy to do yourself. In Canada, the CRA site has great information about registering a business with links to provincial sites. If you live in Ontario or British Columbia, you can use the link at the CRA site to register directly with CRA and also set up your provincial accounts at the same time. For other provinces, there are separate sites which you can easily find with a Google search.

If you are located somewhere else other than North America, conduct careful online searches or visit your local government offices in person to determine the process for properly registering a new business and complying with local tax rules.

Choosing a Business Name & Registering a Domain

If you decide to operate using a business name, spend some time coming up with something unique. Look through supplier pages on nonprofit and voluntary sector resource sites or search using terms a client might use and see what names some companies are already operating under. Once you find a name you like, check what domains are available for that name. Once you successfully register your chosen name, you will want to purchase a domain address for your new business. When you set up your domain account, don't purchase web site hosting just yet, but do set up an email account using your new domain address. This looks much more professional than using Hotmail or Gmail email addresses. Use those free accounts for your personal mail, and set up a separate account for your business email. However, if you are not ready to purchase a domain, choose a Gmail account with your company name or service as part of the address so that you can keep your business and personal email messages separate.

Sales Taxes

I'm not going to get into too much detail on sales tax for each province or state in your country, but I'll give you a quick overview to help you understand how it works for small business providers. Government information tends to be overly complicated and this might make things less intimidating for you. Here is a step-by-step process of how sales collection and remittance works.

- When you bill your clients, always quote your services as your fee *plus* sales tax.

- On your invoices, you must note your sales tax registration number and include a calculation for the tax that is owing.

- When you receive payment from your client, I would recommend that you put an amount equivalent to the sales tax amount into a separate savings account. You can then be sure that you have the funds available to remit the tax to the taxman at the end of the year. You will not have to remit all of it, but a good portion of it so better to have the cash flow ready.

- When you set up your sales tax account, you can elect

to either file a sales tax return quarterly or annually. I would recommend that you file annually since it is less paperwork.

- However, even though you might file annually, after the first year of operations in which you have collected sales tax, you may need to make estimated quarterly payments. This estimate is usually based on what you paid in tax in the previous year.

- At the end of the year, you will file a sales tax annual return. The amount of sales tax that you return to the government is reduced slightly by the tax that you pay out of pocket on legitimate business expenses. These are referred to as "tax credits."

Record-keeping for Tax Purposes

If you have any salaried payroll employment throughout the year, you will receive the usual tax statement from your employer and you will file a regular income tax return. As a small business owner, in addition to your regular return, you will include some additional schedules listing your self-employment income and business expenses. In Canada, the tax form to use is *Form T2125 Statement of Business or Professional Activities.* In the US, the forms will include, at a minimum, *Schedule C Profit or Loss From Business* and *Form 882 Expenses for Business Use of Your Home.* These forms and schedules will list your consulting income, business expenses, and home office and vehicle expenses. In order to complete these forms each year, it's imperative to maintain good record-keeping throughout the year in order to make the process as easy as possible. If you have a large number of expense receipts, it can be a nightmare to organize everything. Here is a list of the most common items you will need to track throughout the year. You can do this using an Excel spreadsheet or software like Quickbooks or an online system such as Kashoo. Keep and store all of your receipts in a file marked with the taxation year for at least seven years after filing.

Income & Business Expenses:

Invoices sent to clients and amounts paid

Advertising expenses

Meals with clients

Business memberships & subscriptions

Office expenses

Equipment & Furniture purchases

Legal & Accounting costs

Business bank account interest & fees

Subcontractor expenses

Convention, seminar & training expenses

Cellphone, landline & Internet expenses

Home Office:

Home heating & electricity costs

Mortgage Interest & Property Taxes – if homeowner

Maintenance fees – if condo owner

Rent paid – if renting

Vehicle Costs:

Vehicle mileage (record year end mileage each year)

Gas and oil costs

Car maintenance & repairs

Car Insurance

Licence & Registration expenses

Lease payments OR Interest costs

Purchase price of car and dates of purchase/sale

Banking

Once you have decided on a name for your company—of if you plan to use your own name—you should consider opening up a business bank account. People who are self-employed often raise the suspicion of the taxman since there are many people who set up fake businesses in order to benefit from tax deductions. You want to do everything possible to avoid those kinds of problems. If you separate your business and personal transactions as much as possible, then if you ever get audited, it will be easy to show the business-related transactions in your business bank account and this may help you avoid having to show your personal information. Deposit all of your client cheques into your business account and pay for your business expenses from this account. Make transfers to your personal account as needed to pay yourself.

Setting Up a Home Office

If you plan to hold yourself out as a professional consultant, you need to have a well-equipped office. It doesn't make sense to rent commercial space unless you absolutely have no room in your home. Your clients will not meet you at your office, so as long as you have a private, comfortable work area, it makes more sense to set up a home office. Ideally, you'll want a separate room where you can close the door if needed for phone meetings or focused privacy. An extra bedroom or finished basement area is ideal. If you do need to rent outside your home, consider locating shared commercial spaces, which are more economical. Whatever space you locate, you'll need enough room for a large desk with a good ergonomic chair, some cabinet and bookshelf storage, and the appropriate tech equipment. If you can afford it, purchase both a desktop and laptop computer. A laptop is critical since you will be travelling to client sites. You can also use a laptop hooked up to a larger monitor and keyboard if you can't afford to purchase a separate desktop. Whether you use an Apple system or Windows, make sure you purchase Microsoft Office software (Word, Excel, Powerpoint) since most businesses use these formats for document production. The second most important piece of equipment is a good laser printer— preferably one with scan capability. A fax machine is not really necessary in this business. If possible, purchase a printer that prints both black and white and colour. However, if you can't afford the cost of a colour printer, you can easily get colour documents printed at the big-box business supply stores. Whatever printer you buy, make sure it is laser and not ink-jet.

Invoicing

A terrific online system that I use for invoicing clients is Freshbooks (www.freshbooks.com). You can get a free account for up to 3 clients, or a monthly account for $15 a month. It's a great tool because it has a time tracking system for recording time spent each day on different clients. At the end of the month, you generate an invoice for each client and email the invoice to them. At the end of the year, you can print a report showing all of your invoices and income collected which is great for tax purposes. There are other decent online invoicing systems that probably have similar features.

If you decide to create manual invoices, you can set something up in Word or Excel. Invoices should have these elements included:

- Your name or company name and address
- Client name and address
- Invoice number
- Fee charged, description, taxes and total due
- Your sales tax identifier number
- Terms of payment (due in 30 days, due upon receipt, etc.)

Logo, Stationery & Business Cards

As a consultant, you'll need to have business cards and possibly a bit of letterhead and envelope stationary. Check out vistaprint.com for an inexpensive option. If you'd like to create a logo, you can hire a designer to create something for you for under $500. An inexpensive option is an online logo maker such as logomaker.com and many others which produce logos for under $50 or even free. Another site to check out is fiverr.com where you can find designers who will create inexpensive logos for you.

Insurance

As long as you do not have any employees working for you, you will not need Workers Compensation coverage. However, you might want to consider Errors and Omissions insurance. This type of insurance protects you from lawsuits claiming that your consulting advice caused harm to a client. If you are a member of a trade association, see if they offer group insurance plans and take advantage of those savings.

CHAPTER TWELVE
How To Respond to an RFP

A Request for Proposal or "RFP" for short, is the most common type of tender for work process that you will likely encounter. There are also two other formats: RFI – Request for Information or RFQ – Request for Quote. These formats are not as commonly used in the voluntary sector because the RFP is more formal. It's a request for specific information such as how the consultant will identify the problem and what methodology will they use to address it. This is the kind of information that organizations are looking for to compare and contrast among vendors.

Proposal writing can be time-consuming so it's a good idea to develop a template or standard format that you will use. That way you can plug in the information required and won't have to spend too much time formatting every time you do a proposal. There are a few general sections that should be addressed, but note that the RFP itself will provide clues as to what areas you should focus on. The RFP will also specify when and if questions can be submitted to the client. It's important to note these details and respect the client's instructions to the letter.

RFP Sections

Here are a few of the general categories or sections that should be included when drafting a proposal along with some general descriptions:

Project Purpose

Re-state the project requirements from the RFP. Elaborate here to show your full understanding of the business case and what is required.

Scope of Work

This is a general statement that describes the work to be done.

Relevant Experience

This section should be a standard statement about your background and experience, but customized to address the client's sector and/or requirements. The more you customize, the better chance you will have of making a case for yourself as the best consultant for the job.

Key Deliverables

List the specific items you will complete and deliver to the client. This will usually be either deliverables requested in the RFP or—if not spelled out—reports or other documents, presentations to leadership, or any other deliverables that you know will flow from the requirements of the job or task.

Methodology & Framework

This section forms the meat of the proposal and is one of the most important sections. Here you will illustrate what approach you will take to carry out the work step by step. Include any specific methodology such as SWOT analysis, document review, competitive review, interviews, strategies, tactics, key performance indicators, financial issues, etc.

Assumptions/Requirements

This section details anything that you require from the client in order to carry out the work. For example, if you are doing a document review, you would want to note that it would be the client's responsibility to gather all the documents to be provided to you. To identify these items, simply think about what work is involved and your steps to carry that out. If there is some background work or supplies needed, be sure to spell that out so there is no confusion later.

Timelines

List approximate timelines or start and completion dates, depending on the RFP. Include a table with activity and approximate dates if you feel that level of detail is necessary at this stage.

Contracting

Note what contracting documents will be required. Pull from the RFP or if the RFP is silent on this, include what you think makes sense such as a Statement of Work (SOW), a Service Level Agreement, a Confidentiality Agreement, etc.

Project Primaries & Supports

If you are operating under a business name and you've spoken about your company under Relevant Experience above, you should then include your name here as the principal consultant with a paragraph or two from your CV.

Or you could also attach your entire CV and reference that here. If you are partnering with other consultants or administrative support, list those names here and identify each person's role in the project.

Fees for Services

This is where you will provide your quotation for the work. Check the RFP to see if they are looking for an hourly rate with estimated hours to produce the required deliverables or if they are asking for a flat project fee. This section is where you might also note how you will invoice the client along with the terms of payment.

Successful Proposal Writing

In the course of drafting your proposal, if you find some serious gaps of missing information, you can usually reach out to the client to answer a few questions. Read the RFP carefully and find out if there is a formal process for receiving questions and follow that process carefully. You don't want to annoy the client or communicate in a way that they specifically asked people not to. If no information is provided, then you can usually outline your questions in an email to the client.

With every RFP, there are likely some aspects to the work requirements that go either slightly or largely beyond your scope. You'll have no problem addressing elements within your core skills, but if there are new processes or methodologies involved, you'll need to conduct some background research. In this day and age, for consultants, the Internet is a valuable resource. If you are not already skilled at mining the Internet for information, you'll soon become an expert.

Your first step should be to get onto the client's website and read anything and everything you can about mission, activities, organizational structure, finances—whatever you can find online. Also do some reading on the sector if you don't already know it well enough to speak intelligently to it. Depending on the kind of work you'll be doing as a consultant, you may need to drill down deeper into functional areas such as the organization's existing marketing, events or project work. A good document to read if they include it as a download on their website, is the most recent Annual Report. This document will include a ton of information such as board members, financials, project work, and activity outcomes.

Along with reviewing client information online, your next source of information might be related to methodologies or work processes in the particular area you plan to consult on. For example, if you are working with a client on developing a strategic planning process, you will want to validate your methodology, read any current best practices, or flesh out a new approach that might work well for this particular client. Many of the larger consulting agencies or research organizations publish process documents and innovative ideas that you can incorporate into your proposal.

If the project is fairly large in scope and there are some gaps in what you are able to deliver, keep in mind that you can subcontract other freelancers to assist you on the project. In some cases, your proposal might be written as a partnership or a team engagement. An alternative approach is to speak to everything required in the proposal and indicate to the client that you will outsource some activities such as graphic design or web development. In either case, you will need to ask the freelancer for some background information to include in the proposal or, as above, research those areas to familiarize yourself with what is involved and to be able to write about the tasks in the proposal.

Once completed, your proposal should of course be neatly and professionally prepared with absolutely no typos or grammatical errors. If you are not a good proofreader, you may need to hire someone to look over your proposals for you. If you have a logo, include it on the first page and then number successive pages. Also draft a cover letter introducing yourself, the RFP name or file number, and reference your attached proposal. Email or mail as requested in the RFP instructions. Both your cover letter and the first page of your proposal should include your full contact details.

Another thing to keep in mind when preparing a proposal is to provide just enough information on your methodology and approach to address the client's need without going in to too much detail. You don't want to give away all of your proprietary methods before getting paid for your expertise.

A final word of advice: beware of RFP's that have a quick deadline. Not only is it difficult to respond on short notice, but quite often this is a sign that the organization has already chosen an agency to handle the work. Because of internal procurement policies, they may be required to put out a tender for the work. As a result, your chances of winning a contract where the organization already has a preferred agency is slim. If you have any knowledge of the tendering organization or any connections to staff, try to find out if there is a preferred agency or consultant. If so, you might want to take a pass and avoid putting in a lot of work on a proposal for nothing.

Getting Short-listed

Depending on the size and scope of the client work, you might go through a short-list process and a secondary proposal stage which will include an in-person meeting or presentation. This usually means that the client is interviewing more than one potential consultant. When you get this call from the client, try to find out if the meeting will be informal—with just one person—or with a panel of individuals. Get the names and job titles of everyone who will be involved so you can start preparing your preparation. You can also ask whether you are the only candidate or competing with others at this stage.

If you are the only candidate and the meeting is one-on-one with the client, you probably don't need to do much more preparation than reviewing the client's website, the RFP, and your proposal—prior to the meeting. You might want to bring some references along in case the client asks for those. If applicable, also bring hardcopy samples of past client work.

If the project is fairly large in scope and the meeting is with a panel of two or more people AND especially if you are competing with other consultants for the work, then it's important to prepare a more formal presentation. This should include a slide presentation using PowerPoint. It doesn't need to be very long, but it should include a few slides that take the interview panel through your proposal in a clear way. If the work you are doing is creative—such as marketing or events management—your presentation should reflect your creativity. In addition to the presentation, you might bring some handouts that support the work you plan to do or examples of past client work (if applicable). If you are partnering with any other consultants or sub-contractors, consider having them attend the presentation with you in order to add extra fire power to the formal proposal. Be prepared to answer questions and expand on your proposal in a way that will sell you as the best consultant for the job.

CHAPTER THIRTEEN
Knowing What to Charge

One of the burning questions new consultants have is knowing what to charge for their services. There are basically two different ways to propose fees to a client—billing based on an hourly rate or billing based on a project rate. If using a project rate, you will still estimate the number of hours it should take to complete the project multiplied by the hourly or daily rate you generally charge for that service.

Another optional (although lesser-known) approach is known as "outcome-based" or "value-based" fees. Together with a client, you would determine what the total value of the project is, and based on that value, you would then establish a fee that is commensurate with your contribution to the success of the project. This eliminates the hassle of time tracking. The benefit to both parties is that you can spend as much time as needed to meet the project objectives. For the client, there are no billing surprises.

No matter which approach you take to fee billing, there will often be times where the project changes scope (referred to as "project creep") or the client asks for something that wasn't in the original proposal. Your job as a consultant is to keep the client informed whenever billing might go beyond what was agreed upon. Finances are always a big consideration for nonprofits and charities so it's best to be upfront about costs. On the other hand, you don't want to always be penny-pinching and there may be some situations where you simply get the job done and absorb any extra cost. This is a judgment call that needs to be finessed by you based upon each different situation so that you balance your own needs with building good customer relations.

Billing by the hour works well when a project is open-ended; for example, handling ongoing web content management for a nonprofit or writing a weekly blog post. When initially quoting on the work, you should estimate how much time it will take you to do the task and agree with the client on a maximum limit. That way the client will know you are respecting their budget and won't have to worry about receiving a bill at the end of the month with exorbitant hours. As you work, you should track your time and detail the hours to the client in your invoicing.

Project billing makes sense when the work is time-limited. When you initially quote on the work, you will need to carefully work out the scope of the project, the steps involved, and how much time you estimate it will take you to complete. This is helpful not only for the billing side of things, but for working through your proposal and methodology. You can do this on a spreadsheet and note down as much detail as possible because this worksheet is not something you will show to the client. This is for your calculations only. You should also add in any additional subcontracting you might require if you need to bring in other consultants on the project. Include other vendors and services such as graphic designers or printers. Also estimate the number of on-site client meetings required and your travel time to and from these meetings. Multiply the total work hours by the hourly rate for each type of task. You may have a single hourly rate or day rate that you charge, or you might have a different rate depending on the type of work you are doing. Things like writing and editing work are generally lower cost than strategy consulting, for example.

The starting point for any project and the best way to work out cost, is to simply ask the client what their budget is for the project. If the number is extremely low and you know you would not be able to do the work, try to ask more questions so you understand what the client's needs are. If the number seems reasonable, your response should be, "I can work within that budget." In most cases, the budget figure is much higher than you expected. In that case, you have an opportunity to earn more than you might have thought by delivering the right level of service to come in just under their maximum budget figure.

In other situations, an RFP will tell you up front what the budget is for a particular project. In this situation, you will still do your careful estimate of the scope and time involved, and you will see whether you can do the work comfortably within the client's budget. If so, then it is best to come in slightly under budget on your quote. If the budget is extremely low, and you still want to bid on the work, you will need to condense some of the work processes and scale back where necessary while still providing a useful deliverable for the client. Sometimes you simply want to get your foot in the door with a client and you may be willing to do a job for less than you might normally charge. Or it may be a cause that is near and dear to your heart. As a consultant you can decide what work you want to take on and what work doesn't make sense for you. Over time, you may have a range of low paying clients and higher paying clients. Your goal is to hang on to the clients you enjoy working for the most—whose work is rewarding to you—and ideally, who pay you the best.

Consulting Rates

So let's get to specifics and talk about typical rates. Rates in the nonprofit and charity sector for consultants are lower than consulting rates in the for-profit sector so be aware of this difference if you hear other amounts quoted for consulting rates. Currently, typical rates in North America range between $45 per hour on the low end to $125 per hour at the upper end of the scale. Daily rates range from $400 to $1,000. The low end of these rates would apply to a junior consultant. Mid-range rates around $80 to $100 per hour are the average and most common rates quoted. Higher end rates of $125 and $1,000 per day would apply to seasoned senior consultants, skilled group facilitators, and strategic management consultants.

Getting Paid

There are different ways to arrange payment and this should be spelled out in your proposal. If your agreement is to bill hourly, then it makes sense to produce an invoice at the end of each month detailing the hours you worked and what you did for the client. If payment is project-based, you may want to ask for a deposit up front with interim payments at designated milestones. Final payment would be made on any balance remaining at the completion of the last deliverable. In some cases where organizations are working within fiscal period budgets, you may be asked to adjust your billing so that invoices are received before period ends. You may get paid earlier than you expected because the organization needs to spend the money allocated to your project within a certain timeframe.

CHAPTER FOURTEEN
So You Won the RFP, Now What?

So you wrote a killer proposal and got short-listed by an organization. A couple of weeks ago they asked you to provide more specifics in writing. Today, you got the call that you've been selected for the work. Congratulations! Good job! So now what happens?

The next step in the process is to document the contractual arrangement and work to be done in a Statement of Work— known as an "SOW" for short or a Service Agreement. The documents required will depend on the organization and also on the size of the project. Before preparing these documents though, you will likely have one or two meetings with the client by phone or in person. The proposal process is a blind one in a lot of respects. Once you know you'll be doing the work, you will have a number of questions to more accurately flesh out your work processes. Be sure to ask as many questions as possible to clarify and solidify the work to be done. Ensure that your quoted fees are appropriate to the work and negotiate any adjustments that might be required as a result of new information. Once all of this is clear, determine whether you or the client will prepare the agreements. I have had it happen both ways—generally government agencies will prepare the documents. Smaller nonprofits and charities are happy to have me do it.

The following are typical clauses included in a Service Agreement:

- Names and contact information for both parties – client and consultant

- Term of the agreement (time period)

- Description of deliverables and scope of work to be done

- Intellectual Property clause

- Confidentiality and Nondisclosure clause

- Termination clause

- Indemnification clause

- Fees to be paid

- Invoicing procedures and terms of payment

- Signatures and dates

See the template sample at the end of this chapter for an example for a small project managing the redesign of a website.

A Statement of Work is often used for a larger, more complex project and can be quite lengthy. Keep in mind that a large organization will likely need a business case to get financing approval for the work, so an SOW is typically used by them to secure that funding within their department.

Here are a few possible sections that might be included in an SOW:

- Background and Business Case

- Recommended Approach

- Project Objectives

- Work Phases & Deliverables

- Total Budget Estimate

- Payment Schedule

- Timelines & Milestones

Once any agreements have been approved or signed off on, the work can begin. In fact, as soon as you know you will be awarded the work, it's pretty safe to begin doing any background reading or research so you can hit the ground running with the client. Track the time you spend on these activities and consider it billable work. Schedule your first meeting with the client as soon as possible.

SERVICE AGREEMENT

Client: Village Animal Shelter
Contact: Jessica Jones
Project: Project Management of Website Redesign for
www.villageshelter.com

Scope of Services:

Carol Austin to provide Independent Consultant services
which will include the following scope of work and
deliverables:

1. Audit existing website
2. Draft project brief
3. Draft sitemap
4. Coordinate development of design assets (with graphic
   designer to be determined)
5. Coordinate programming of new site (with client)
6. Assist with content transfer/upload
7. Coordinate launch of new site (with client)

Timelines:

Project Start: March 2017
Project Brief & Sitemap: April 2017
Design Phase: May 2017
Programming Phase: June 2017
Launch Phase: July 2017

Fee Structure:

$75.00 hourly rate plus tax. I estimate a maximum budget of
$2,000 or approximately 25 hours will be required to
manage the scope of work for this project. This does not
include extensive content uploads or drafting of new content

which would be an extra cost.

Other Fees:
Courier and postage charges, long distance, and any third party expenses extra. (As needed and with prior approval of client.)

Terms and Conditions:
Cancellation - This agreement may be cancelled at any time by client or service provider with 30 days' written notice.
Payment - Invoices will be submitted monthly and are payable upon receipt.
Acceptance of Terms - By signing this retainer of services, the client hereby accepts these terms and conditions, which shall be binding for the duration of service provision.

The parties have duly executed this Service Agreement this _____ day of March, 2017.

_____

Jessica Jones

_____

Carol Austin

CHAPTER FIFTEEN
Doing the Work: How to Be An Exceptional Consultant

In any job or career, you should strive to be exceptional at what you do. A strong work ethic and personal integrity are important traits to foster. This is even more important as a consultant because every client you acquire (especially the good ones) you want to keep for the life of your career. You'll be competing against other consultants, so you want to be sure to stand out as one of the best in your field. From the client's perspective, outsourced services and individual consultants are usually held to a higher standard. The employer doesn't and shouldn't need to groom you or help you develop professionally as they would do with their salaried employees. You should be 100% polished and skilled from the start. Here are a few areas to highlight where you'll want to pay particular attention to as a consultant.

Customer Service

As a consultant, you might be juggling multiple clients, but you need to treat every client as number one. Make sure all your clients can contact you quickly and easily. Respond to calls and emails as fast as possible. If a client emails you a document or a request, respond immediately to confirm receipt of the email. Always go above and beyond. Keep your promises. Meet deadlines. Stay organized. Remember that the client is your boss and pays your bill.

Flexibility

Flexibility means not acting like you know everything, especially when first walking into a client situation. Allow for an organic process to take shape. Always keep an open mind. Enter with fresh ideas, but not with preconceived dogma. You might be working with multiple stakeholders and need to step back and assess how best to incorporate multiple opinions and needs. Your role is to provide support, to advise, and to allow solutions to take shape in a consultative fashion. Don't force your opinions on the client. Every client environment will be unique and you'll be surprised at all the new things you will learn.

Understanding

Make an effort to really understand your clients before coming up with solutions or ideas. Listen attentively. Go beyond what the client thinks. Discern what people are doing well and not so well. Be perceptive.

Knowledge

Keep abreast of changes in the client sector and your area of work. Don't fight change, new trends or technology. Be positive. Be quick to adapt. Keep an eye on the competition at all times. Be resourceful—build up a list of trusted vendors and continue to bring value to your role with a client. This might include other consultants, graphic designers, writers, print houses, or online resources.

Problem Solving

Don't look for blame when an error or problem arises. Fix what is broken and then move forward. Manage your ego and your emotions. Take the blame if necessary. Rise above the crisis, and take the high road. Make friends and colleagues within the client environment, but don't get involved in office politics. Challenge assumptions in a constructive way and help the client uncover any false assumptions they've been working under.

Excellence

And finally, remember that the thing that most often separates a good consultant from a bad consultant is passion and a drive for excellence. Undoubtedly, once you have built up your new consulting career, this will be self-fulfilling. You will have found your dream career. You will wake up every day feeling enthusiastic and passionate about what you do. Your drive for excellence will come naturally as you strive to do the very best you can for your clients.

Good luck in your new career!

Some of My Favorite Online Productivity & Technology Tools

Wunderlist – wunderlist.com - To-do lists and reminder tool.

Evernote – evernote.com - Tool for capturing notes.

Dropbox – dropbox.com - Cloud file storage and sharing.

WordPress – wordpress.com - Website and blogging tool.

Freshbooks – freshbooks.com - Small business accounting and invoicing.

Kashoo – kashoo.com - Accounting software for small businesses.

Wufoo – wufoo.com - Form building tool.

MailChimp – mailchimp.com - Email marketing tool.

Asana – asana.com - Project management tool for teams.

Basecamp - basecamp.com - Project management tool for teams.

Survey Monkey - surveymonkey.com - Online survey developer.